KANJI PAGE LOCATOR

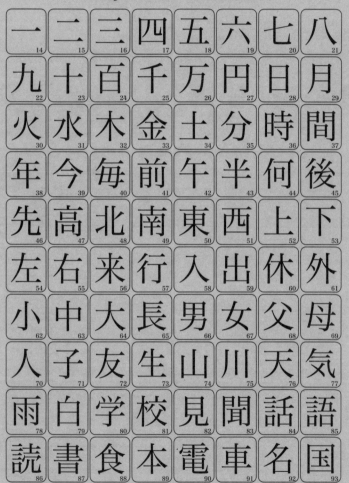

一 14	二 15	三 16	四 17	五 18	六 19	七 20	八 21
九 22	十 23	百 24	千 25	万 26	円 27	日 28	月 29
火 30	水 31	木 32	金 33	土 34	分 35	時 36	間 37
年 38	今 39	毎 40	前 41	午 42	半 43	何 44	後 45
先 46	高 47	北 48	南 49	東 50	西 51	上 52	下 53
左 54	右 55	来 56	行 57	入 58	出 59	休 60	外 61
小 62	中 63	大 64	長 65	男 66	女 67	父 68	母 69
人 70	子 71	友 72	生 73	山 74	川 75	天 76	気 77
雨 78	白 79	学 80	校 81	見 82	聞 83	話 84	語 85
読 86	書 87	食 88	本 89	電 90	車 91	名 92	国 93

MANGA UNIVERSITY presents...

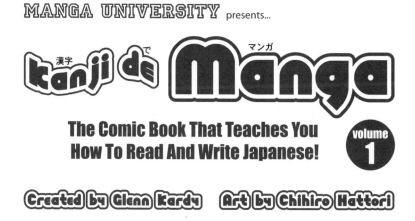

漢字 で マンガ
kanji de Manga

The Comic Book That Teaches You
How To Read And Write Japanese!

volume 1

Created by Glenn Kardy   Art by Chihiro Hattori

Japanime

TOKYO   SAN FRANCISCO

Manga University presents ... Kanji de Manga
The Comic Book That Teaches You
How To Read And Write Japanese!
Volume One

ISBN 4-921205-02-7

Published by Japanime Co. Ltd.
2-8-102 Naka-cho
Kawaguchi-shi
Saitama 332-0022 Japan

First edition
Printed in Japan in December 2004

For our families

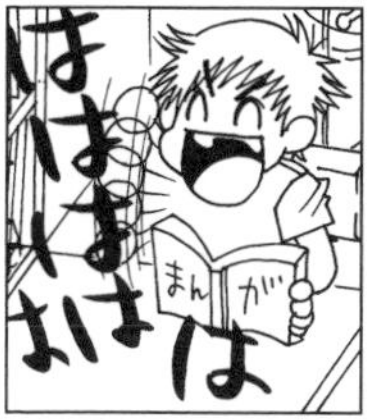
まんが

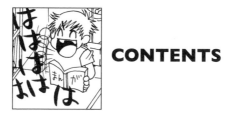

CONTENTS

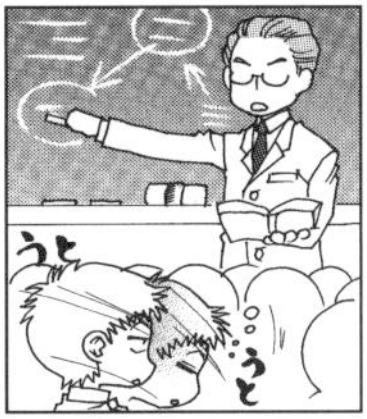
うと
うと

FOREWORD

Students are usually taught that the easiest way to memorize kanji is to think of the characters as little pictures of the objects, actions and ideas they represent. For instance, the kanji for "tree," 木, really does look like a tree trunk with a couple of outstretched branches, and 山 does sort of resemble a mountain.

But what about the hundreds of other everyday kanji you will need to know if you want to read a menu, map or manga in Japanese? Can anyone honestly say 食 really looks like "food," 行 obviously means "to go," or 友 reminds you of a "friend"? So much for simplicity!

"Kanji de Manga" takes a refreshingly different approach. Instead of relying on tired, outdated memory aids, the authors introduce kanji in an exciting format millions of young people can't seem to get enough of: Japanese comics. Each page features a manga drawing with fun dialog showing a single kanji character "in action." An English translation of the comic strip helps reinforce the reader's vocabulary, stroke order is demonstrated step-by-step, and useful compounds are also provided.

By learning how to read and write the 80 kanji presented in this volume, you will have taken the first step toward mastering the Japanese writing system. So don't bother with the "little pictures." Look at the BIGGER pictures—the manga on the pages of this exciting book—and memorize kanji today!

Tomonori Morikawa, Ph.D.
Professor, School of International Liberal Studies
Waseda University
Tokyo, Japan

INTRODUCTION

When you opened this book, you opened the doorway to a new frontier. That frontier is kanji, and it holds the key to reading and writing the Japanese language.

At first, these characters may look difficult, mysterious and even a little intimidating. But "Kanji de Manga" is here to help sort it all out for you in a simple, fun way.

There are nearly 50,000 kanji. You could literally spend a lifetime learning kanji and still not know every character. But don't give up hope just yet. Even most native speakers of Japanese know only a fraction of these 50,000 kanji by heart.

In fact, Japanese students are required to learn just 2,000 of those characters. You need to know only about half of those to read the typical Japanese newspaper—and even less than that to be able to read your favorite manga books in the original Japanese.

Of course, that still leaves plenty to learn, especially when you compare all those characters to the mere 26 letters of the English alphabet. But "Kanji de Manga" contains everything you need to get started, and hopefully you'll have a little fun along the way, too.

By the time you reach the end of this book, you'll be able to read and write the 80 kanji featured in Level 4, the most basic level, of the Japanese Language Proficiency Test. (For more information about the test, please see page 94.) These are the same characters studied in Japan by first- and second-grade students, and include some of the most common and important kanji that you will need to know.

Before we begin, let's take a quick look at the origins of kanji.

Kanji is based on the ancient Chinese writing system. In many cases, these characters are still in use today in China. But don't try to learn both languages at once: While some kanji share the same meaning in both languages, many do not, and the sentence structures of the two languages are profoundly different.

Most kanji have at least two common pronunciations: a purely Japanese pronunciation, called kun-yomi, and one based on the original Chinese, called on-yomi. The Japanese began borrowing kanji many centuries ago, so the on-yomi pronunciations—Japanese versions of Middle Chinese—usually sound very different from the modern Chinese pronunciation of each character.

You will find both pronunciations in this book. Like many Japanese-language textbooks, we will show you the kun-yomi in hiragana and on-yomi in katakana. And if you haven't gotten your hiragana and katakana down yet, don't worry—simply get out your copy of "Kana de Manga" for a quick refresher.

You may have noticed that we said that each character has *at least* two pronunciations. Some characters have even more. Many of those are obscure and seldom-used pronunciations, and we have omitted them from this lesson to help move things along. You won't miss them!

Even when we narrow each character down to its two most common pronunciations, figuring out whether to use the on-yomi or kun-yomi can still be tricky. At first, it may seem random and unstructured. And, in some ways, it is.

But soon you'll begin to notice some trends. Compound words, or words made up of multiple kanji, are generally read using the on-yomi pronunciation. Kanji occurring in isolation, or next to only kana characters, are generally read using the kun-yomi pronunciation. Japanese place names and family names also tend to be pronounced using the kun-yomi pronunciations.

There are, of course, exceptions—and plenty of them. In fact, the very name of the country—Japan—is read using the on-yomi pronunciation: "Nihon," or 日本 in kanji. And when it comes to given names, even native speakers often need a little help trying to figure it all out.

But don't be daunted. The task may be difficult, and the journey long, but with "Kanji de Manga" as your guide, you'll also find it rewarding and fun.

So let's get started on the journey of a lifetime—a journey into the magical world of Japanese culture. And when you are ready to graduate to the next level, "Kanji de Manga" will be ready to take the next step with you with our more advanced lessons.

Ready? Set? Gambatte!

PAGE GUIDE

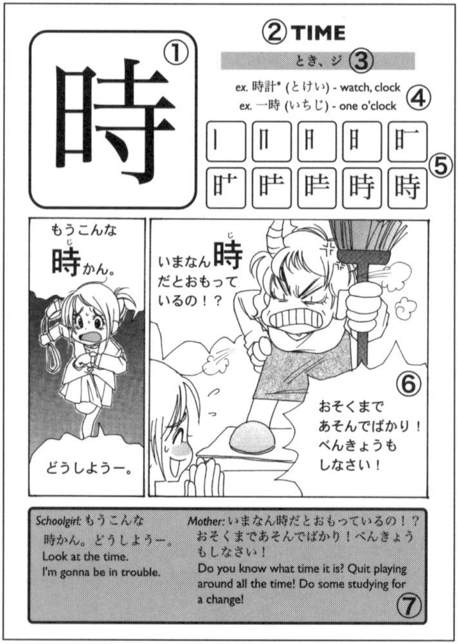
時
①
② TIME
とき、ジ ③
ex. 時計* (とけい) - watch, clock
ex. 一時 (いちじ) - one o'clock ④
⑤
もうこんな時かん。
どうしようー。
いまなん時だとおもっているの！？
⑥
おそくまであそんでばかり！べんきょうもしなさい！
Schoolgirl: もうこんな時かん。どうしようー。
Look at the time.
I'm gonna be in trouble.
Mother: いまなん時だとおもっているの！？おそくまであそんでばかり！べんきょうもしなさい！
Do you know what time it is? Quit playing around all the time! Do some studying for a change!
⑦

① The featured kanji

② Common definition

③ Readings: kun-yomi (Japanese readings) are written in hiragana, while on-yomi (Chinese readings) are in katakana.

④ Examples of compounds containing the featured kanji, their pronunciations (written in hiragana) and English definitions. (An asterisk next to a compound indicates that one or more of its kanji are not featured in this volume of the "Kanji de Manga" series.)

⑤ Stroke order: In general, the strokes are written from top to bottom and left to right. For a list of additional stroke-order rules, please refer to the chart at the back of this book.

⑥ The manga. All dialogue is written in hiragana and katakana except for the single featured kanji. The proper pronunciation of the kanji is indicated in furigana (tiny hiragana) written above the character.

⑦ Translation of the dialogue and selected onomatopoeia.

Kanji de Manga

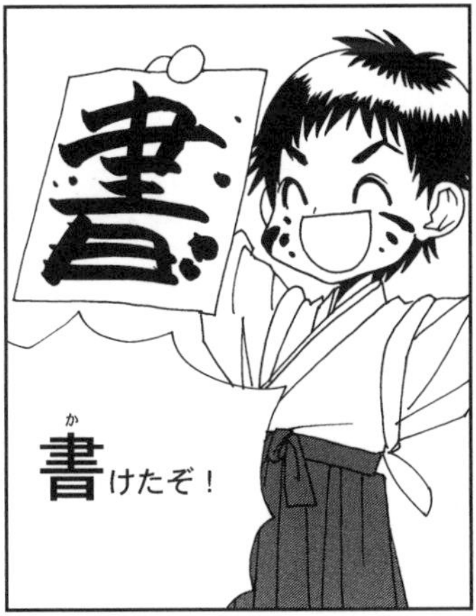
書
書けたぞ！

STUDY SECTION

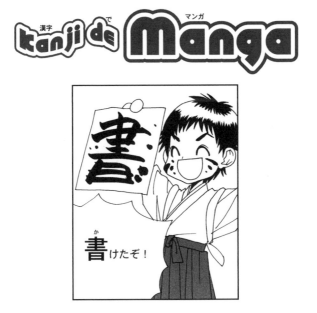

一

ONE

ひと、ひと(つ)、イチ、イッ

ex. 一つ (ひとつ) - one (object)

ex. 一月 (いちがつ) - January

一				

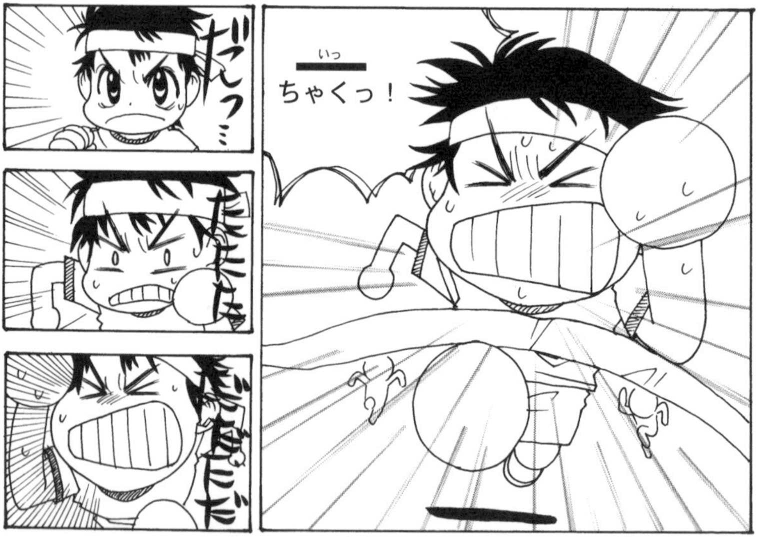
だっ
たたた
だだだだ
一(いっ)ちゃくっ！
一

だっ　たたた　だだだだ
(Onomatopoeia for the sound of heavy footsteps or running. Onomatopoeia are very common in the Japanese language and especially in manga, and can be found throughout this book.)

一ちゃくっ！
First place!

TWO

ふた、ふた(つ)、ニ

ex. 一つ (ふたつ) - two (objects)
ex. 二月 (にがつ) - February

一	二			

二

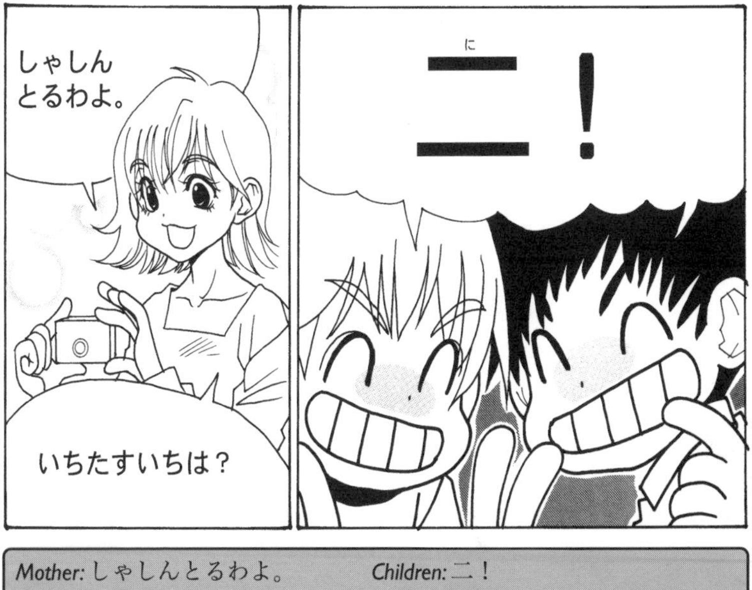
しゃしん
とるわよ。
いちたすいちは？
に
二！

Mother: しゃしんとるわよ。
いちたすいちは？
Time for a photo.
One plus one equals?

Children: 二！
Two!

(In Japan, it is common for children to flash two fingers—in the "V for Victory" sign—when posing for photographs.)

三

THREE

み、み(つ)、みっ(つ)、サン

ex. 三つ (みっつ) - three (objects)

ex. 三月 (さんがつ) - March

一	二	三

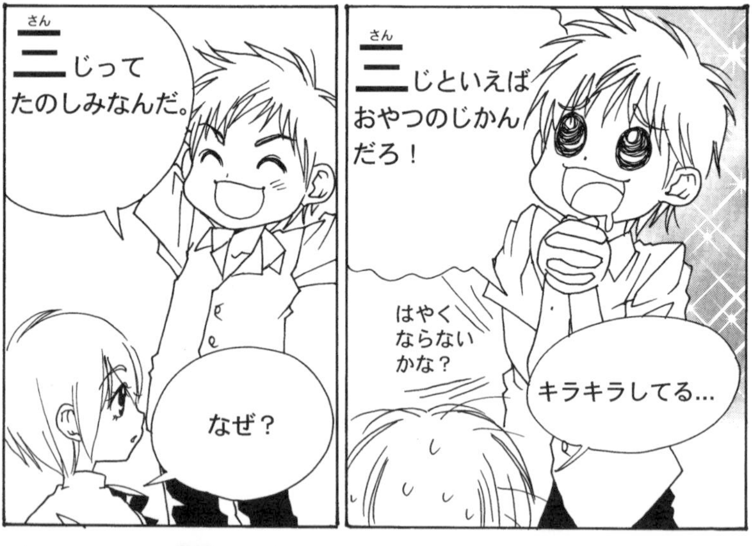
三(さん)じって
たのしみなんだ。
なぜ？
三(さん)じといえば
おやつのじかん
だろ！
はやく
ならない
かな？
キラキラしてる…

Schoolboy: 三じって たのしみなんだ。

I can't wait till 3 o'clock!

Schoolgirl: なぜ？

Why's that?

Schoolboy: 三じといえばおやつの じかんだろ! はやくならないかな？

Because 3 o'clock is snack time!

Is it time yet?

Schoolgirl: キラキラしてる…

There are stars in his eyes...

四

FOUR

よ、よ(つ)、よっ(つ)、よん、シ

ex. 四つ (よっつ) - four (objects)
ex. 四月 (しがつ) - April

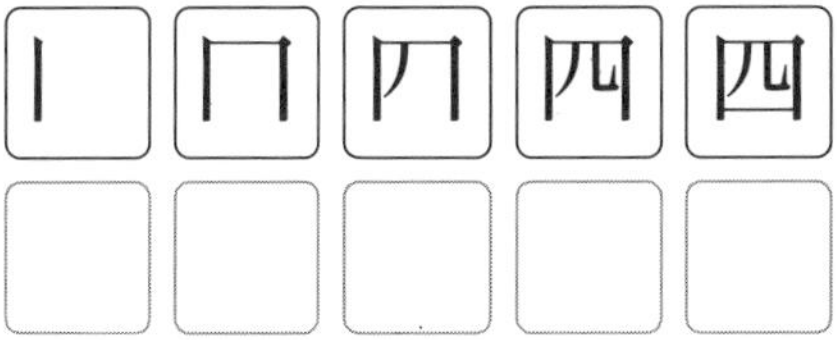

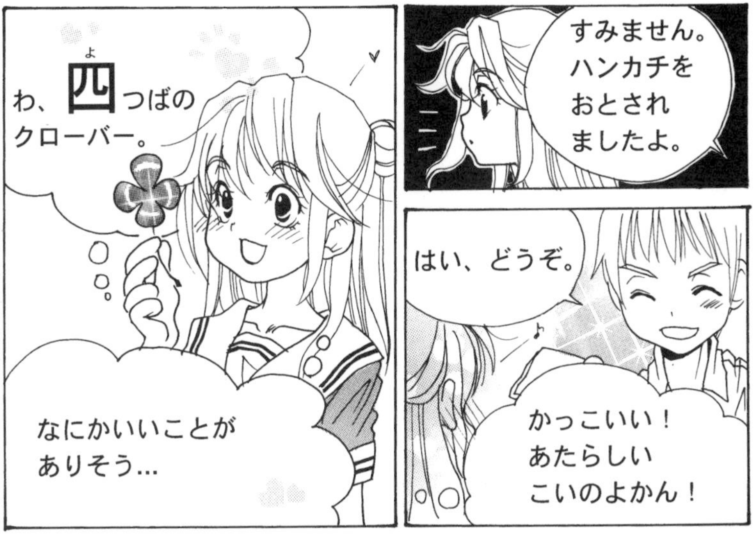
わ、四つばのクローバー。
よ
なにかいいことがありそう…
すみません。ハンカチをおとされましたよ。
はい、どうぞ。
かっこいい！あたらしいこいのよかん！

Girl: わ、四つばのクローバー。なにかいいことがありそう…
Wow, a four-leaf clover! I think I've got some luck heading my way...

Boy: すみません。ハンカチをおとされましたよ。はい、どうぞ。
Excuse me. You dropped your hanky. Here you go.

Girl: かっこいい！あたらしいこいのよかん！
He's so cute! I think I'm in love!

五

FIVE

いつ、いつ(つ)、ゴ

ex. 五つ (いつつ) - five (objects)

ex. 五月 (ごがつ) - May

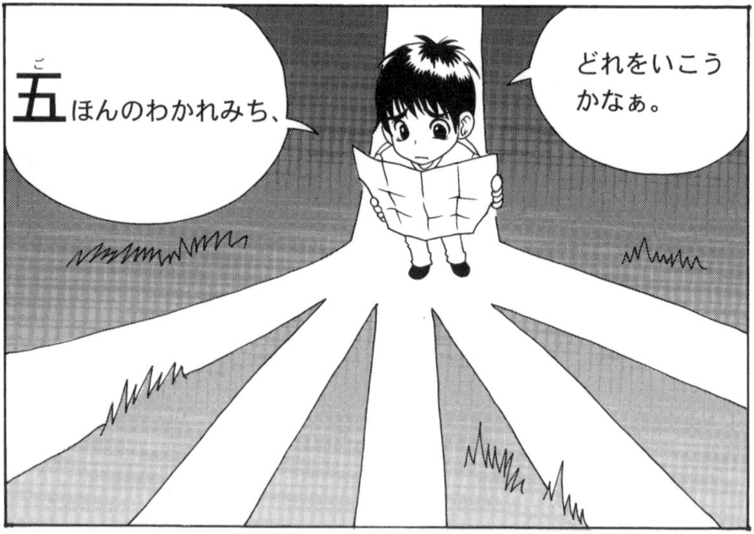
五(ご)ほんのわかれみち、
どれをいこうかなぁ。

Boy: 五ほんのわれみち。

どれをいこうかなぁ。

Five different roads.

Which one should I take?

SIX

六

む、む(つ)、むっ(つ)、むい、ロク

ex. 六つ (むっつ) - six (objects)

ex. 六月 (ろくがつ) - June

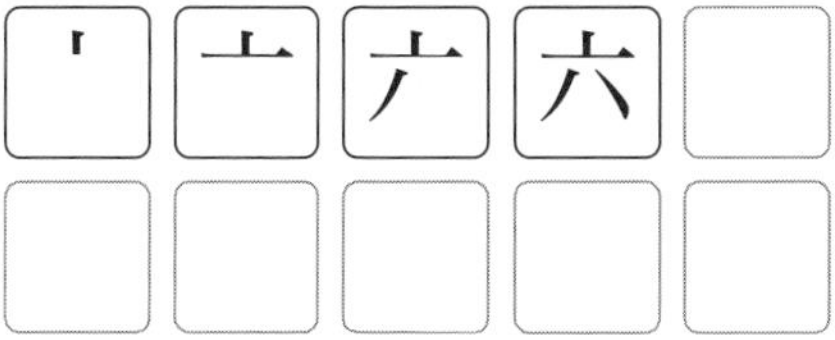

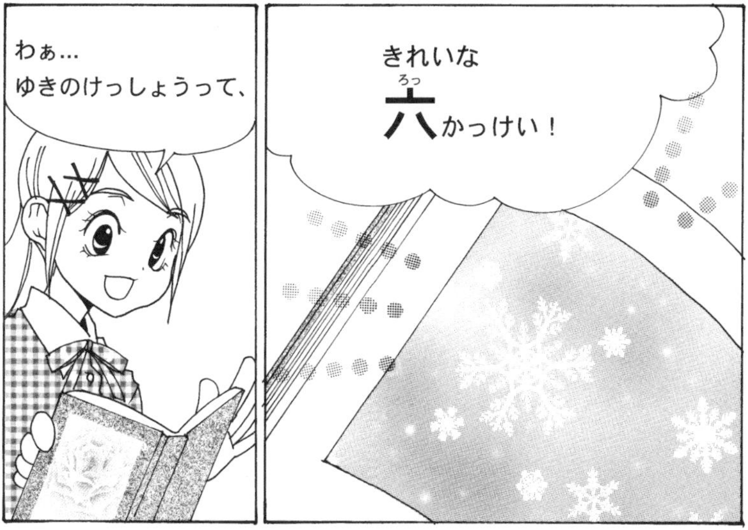
わぁ…
ゆきのけっしょうって、
きれいな
ろっ
六かっけい！

Girl: わぁ… ゆきの
けっしょうって、
Ah, falling snowflakes...

きれいな六かっけい！
...are beautiful hexagons!

七

SEVEN

なな、なな(つ)、なの、シチ

ex. 七つ (ななつ) - seven (objects)

ex. 七月 (しちがつ) - July

一	七			

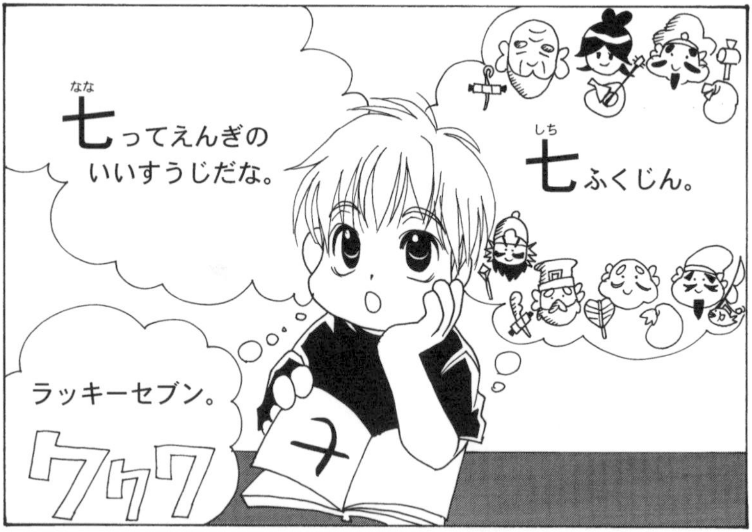
なな
七ってえんぎのいいすうじだな。
しち
七ふくじん。
ラッキーセブン。
ワクワ

Boy: 七ってえんぎのいいすうじだな。

Seven is a lucky number, right?

ラッキーセブン。

Lucky seven.

七ふくじん。

The Seven Gods of Fortune.

(The "Shichifukujin" are Ebisu [god of commerce], Daikokuten [wealth], Bishamonten [warriors], Hotei [abundance], Benzaiten [music] Fukurokuju [wisdom] and Juroujin [longevity].)

EIGHT

や、や(つ)、やっ(つ)、よう、ハチ

ex. 八つ (やっつ) - eight (objects)
ex. 八月 (はちがつ) - August

ノ 八

もうすこし
たべたいけど...

はら八ぶんめっていうし、
やめておこう！
ごちそうさま。
はち

そんなに
たべて？

Boy: もうすこしたべたいけど...
I'd like to eat a bit more, but...

Boy: はら八ぶんめっていうし、
やめておこう！ごちそうさま。
They say a stomach that is only 80%
full is best, so I better stop! Delicious!

Mother: そんなにたべて？
(Only 80% full) after eating all that?

九

NINE

ここの、ここの(つ)、キュウ、ク

ex. 九つ (ここのつ) - nine (objects)
ex. 九月 (くがつ) - September

ノ	九			

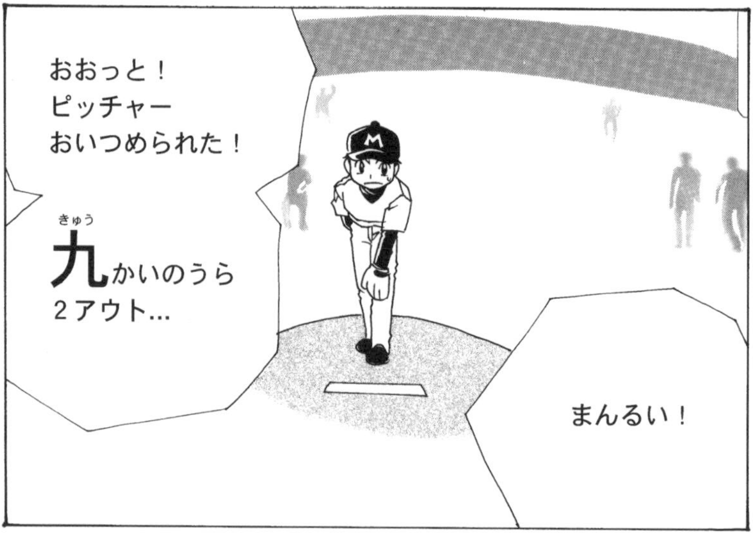
おおっと！
ピッチャー
おいつめられた！
九(きゅう)かいのうら
2アウト…
まんるい！

Radio announcer: おおっと！
ピッチャーおいつめられた！
九かいのうら２アオウト…
The pitcher is in a jam.
Bottom of the 9th, 2 outs...

…まんるい！
...and the bases are loaded!

TEN

十

とお、と、ジュウ、ジッ

ex. 十 (とお) - ten (objects)
ex. 十月 (じゅうがつ) - October

一	十			

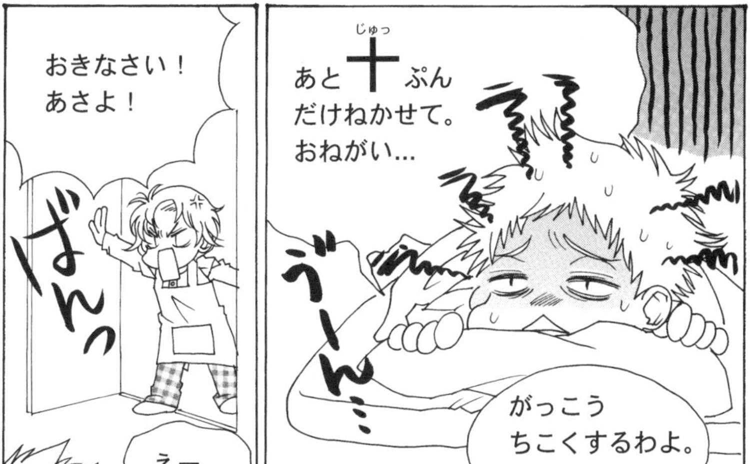
おきなさい！
あさよ！
ばんっ
えー…
あと十(じゅっ)ぷん
だけねかせて。
おねがい…
ゔーん…
がっこう
ちこくするわよ。
おきなさい！

ばんっ (sound of door slam)

Mother: おきなさい！
あさよ！
Wake up! It's morning!

Son: えー…
Huh?

ゔーん (thump)

Son: あと十ぷんだけねかせて。おねがい…
Let me sleep another 10 minutes. Please...

Mother: がっこうちこくするわよ。
おきなさい！
You'll be late for school. Get up now!

HUNDRED

ヒャク、ビャク、ピャク

ex. 百円 (ひゃくえん) - ¥100
ex. 百万 (ひゃくまん) - one million

Babysitter: も…	Babysitter: 百えんまでよ！
Ugh...	OK, but only 100 yen.
Boy: おかしかって、	Boy: わーい！
かって、かってー！	Yay!
Buy me some candy!	

THOUSAND

ち、セン、ゼン

ex. 千年 (ちとせ) - millennium
ex. 千円 (せんえん) - ¥1,000

一 二 千

千

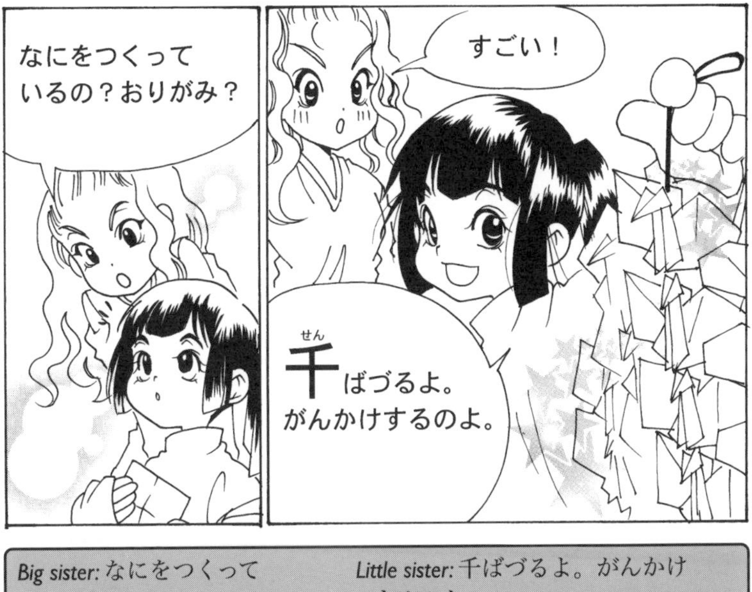
なにをつくって
いるの？おりがみ？
すごい！
千(せん)ばづるよ。
がんかけするのよ。

Big sister: なにをつくっているの？おりがみ？
What are you making? Origami?

Little sister: 千ばづるよ。がんかけするのよ。
I'm making a thousand paper cranes. It's for good luck.

Big sister: すごい！
Wow!

万

TEN THOUSAND

マン、バン

ex. 一万円 (いちまんえん) - ¥10,000
ex. 万国 (ばんこく) - the whole world

一	丂	万		

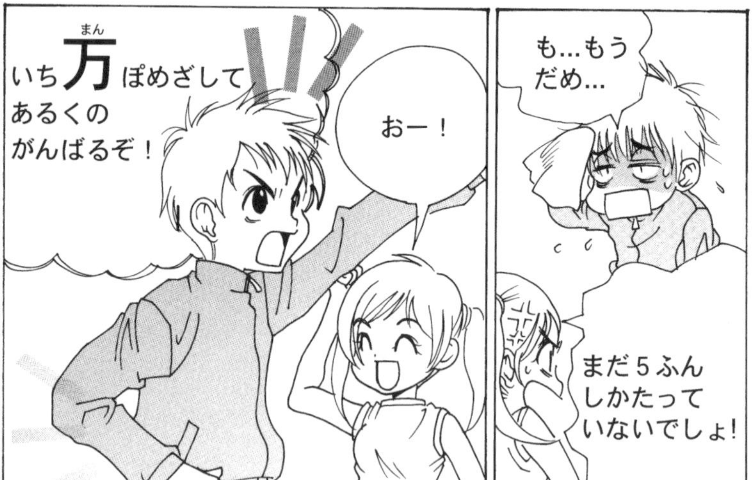
いち万(まん)ぽめざして
あるくの
がんばるぞ！
おー！
も…もう
だめ…
まだ５ふん
しかたって
いないでしょ!

Athlete: いち万ぽめざしてあるくの がんばるぞ！
I'm going to walk 10,000 steps!

Cheerleader: おー！
Right on!

Athlete: も…もうだめ…
That's it...I'm beat...

Cheerleader: まだ５ふんしか たっていないでしょ！
It's only been five minutes!

CIRCLE / YEN

まる(い)、エン

ex. 十円 (じゅうえん) - ¥10
ex. 円い (まるい) - round, circular

丨	冂	冂	円	

円

ごうけい...

2,000 円の
おかいあげです。

Store clerk: ごうけい...2,000円のおかいあげです。
Your total comes to...2,000 yen.

日

SUN / DAY

ひ、か、び、ニチ、ジツ

ex. 日の出 (ひので) - sunrise

ex. 日曜日* (にちようび) - Sunday

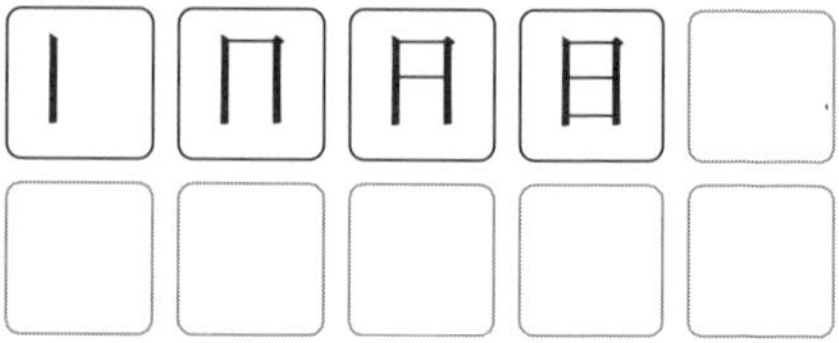

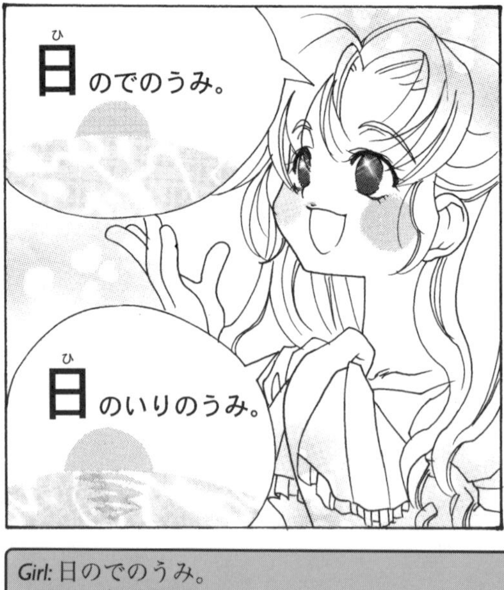
日(ひ)のでのうみ。
日(ひ)のいりのうみ。

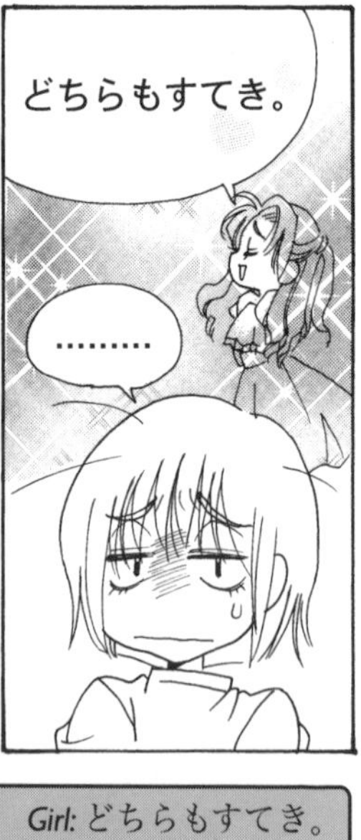
どちらもすてき。
....

Girl: 日のでのうみ。
日のいりのうみ。
Sunrise at the beach.
Sunset at the beach.

Girl: どちらもすてき。
Both are beautiful.

Boy: (speechless)

MOON / MONTH

月

つき、ゲツ、ガツ

ex. 毎月 (まいつき) - every month

ex. 月曜日* (げつようび) - Monday

ノ	冂	月	月	

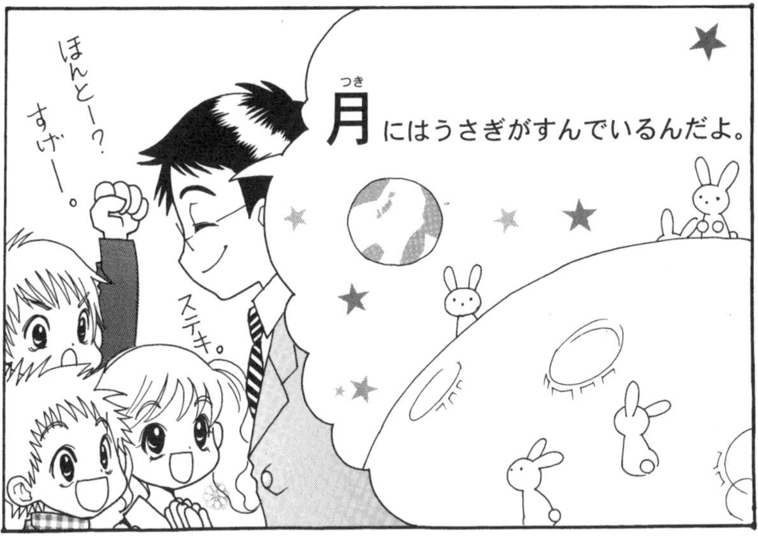
つき
月にはうさぎがすんでいるんだよ。
ほんとー?
すげー。
ステキ。

Father: 月にはうさぎがすんでいるんだよ。

You know, rabbits live on the moon.

Children (in unison): ほんとー？すげー。ステキ。

Really? Wow! How romantic!

(While Westerners say they can see the face of a man on the moon, Japanese claim to see the image of a rabbit making rice cakes.)

火

FIRE

ひ、び、カ

ex. 花火* (はなび) - fireworks
ex. 火曜日* (かようび) - Tuesday

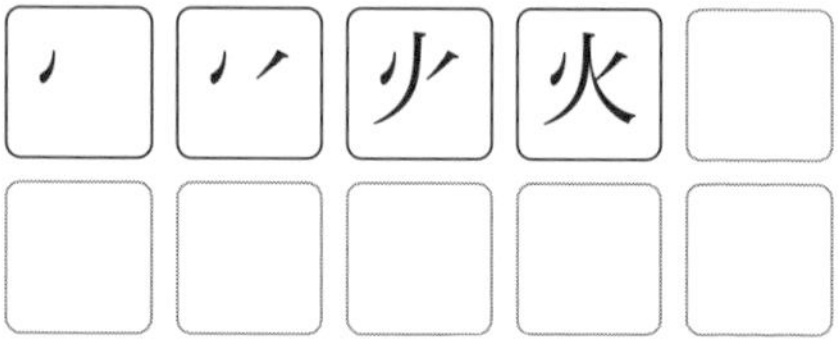

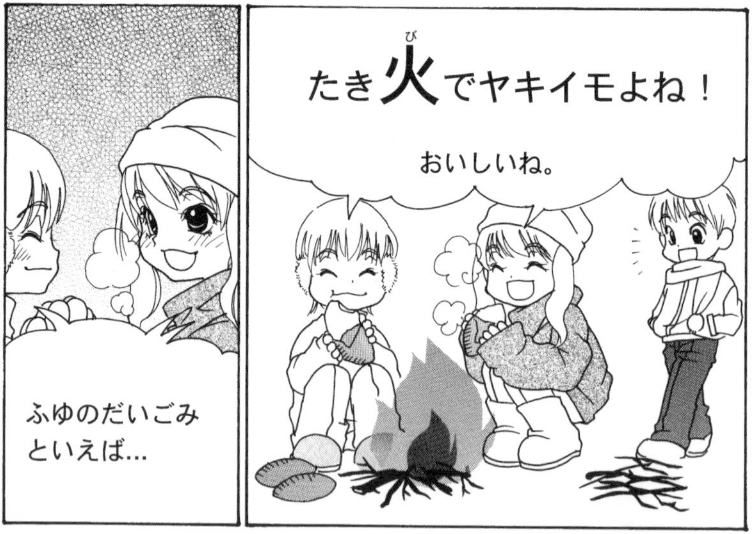
ふゆのだいごみ
といえば...
たき火でヤキイモよね！
おいしいね。

Girl: ふゆのだいごみ
といえば...
The best thing about winter...

Girl: たき火でヤキイモよね！おいしいね。
Roasting sweet potatoes on an open fire!

Boy: おいしいね。
Delicious!

WATER

水

みず、スイ

ex. 飲み水 (のみみず) - drinking water
ex. 水曜日* (すいようび) - Wednesday

亅	才	水	水	

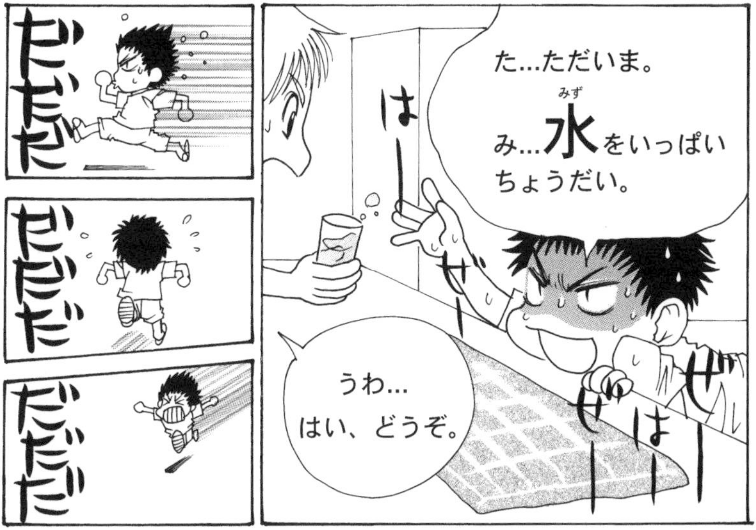
だだだ
だだだ
だだだ
はー
た…ただいま。
み…水をいっぱいちょうだい。
ぜー
うわ…
はい、どうぞ。
ぜー
はー
ぜー
はー

だだだ だだだ だだだ
(sound of heavy running)

ぜーはー ぜーはー ぜーはー (panting)

Boy: た…ただいま。み…水をいっぱいちょだい。

I...I'm home. Gimme lots of wa...water.

Mother: うわ… はい、どうぞ。

Yikes! Here you go!

木

TREE / WOOD

き、ぎ、こ、ボク、モク

ex. 木登り* (きのぼり) - tree-climbing
ex. 木曜日* (もくようび) - Thursday

一	十	オ	木	

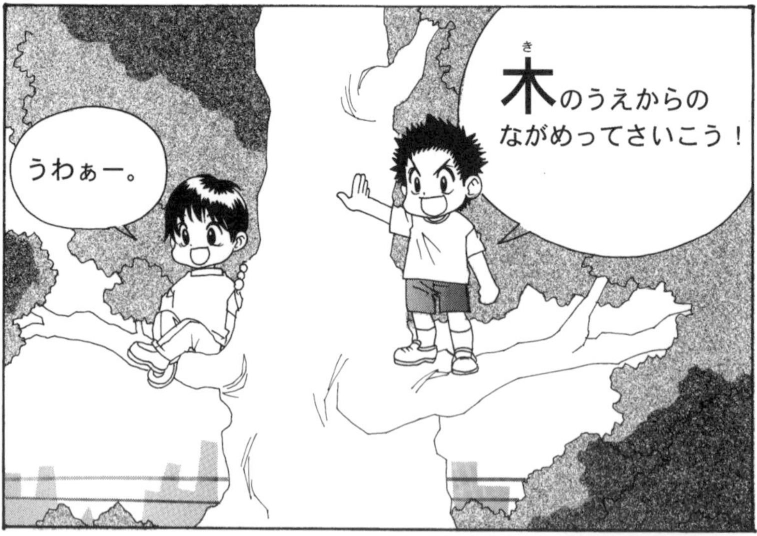
うわぁー。
木(き)のうえからのながめってさいこう！

Boy on left: うわぁー。
Wow!

Boy on right: 木のうえからのながめってさいこう！
The view from the top of this tree is awesome!

GOLD / MONEY

かね、かな、キン、コン

ex. お金 (おかね) - money (polite form)

ex. 金曜日* (きんようび) - Friday

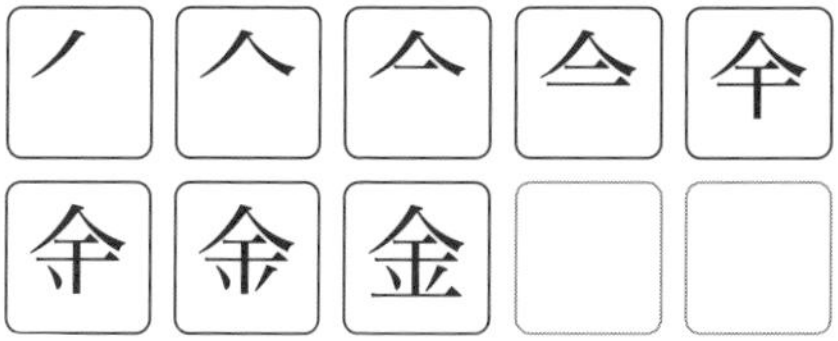

金

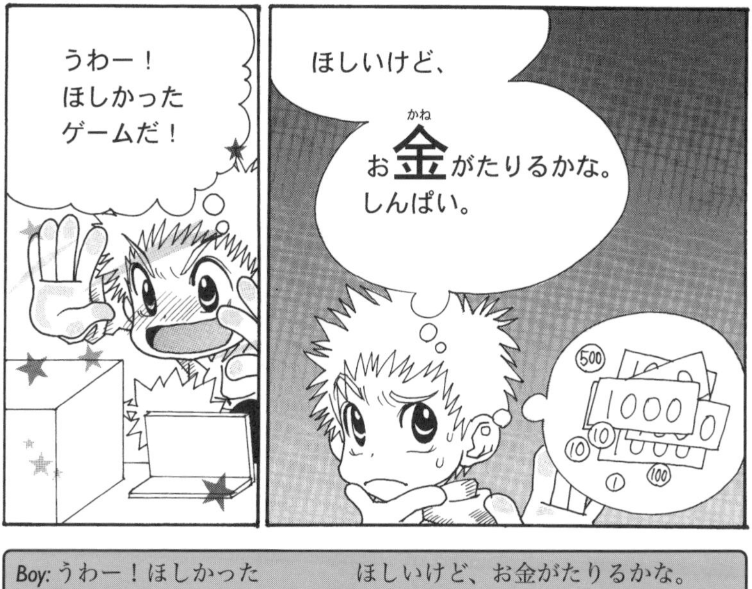
うわー！
ほしかった
ゲームだ！
ほしいけど、
お金がたりるかな。
しんぱい。
500
1000
10
10
10
100
1

Boy: うわー！ほしかった ゲームだ！

Wow! It's that game I've been wanting to buy!

ほしいけど、お金がたりるかな。 しんぱい。

I really want to get it, but I wonder if I have enough money on me.

土

SOIL / GROUND

つち、ド、ト

ex. 土地* (とち) - a plot of land
ex. 土曜日* (どようび) - Saturday

一 十 土

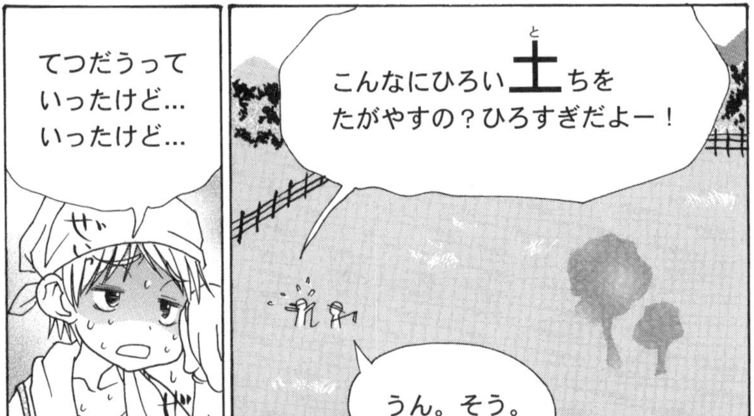
てつだうって
いったけど…
いったけど…
こんなにひろい土ちを
たがやすの？ひろすぎだよー！
うん。そう。

Man: てつだうって
いったけど…
いったけど…
I know I said I'd help, but...

Man: こんなにひろい土ちをたがやすの？
ひろすぎだよー！
We have to plow this whole field?
It's TOO big!

Farmer: うん。そう。
Yep. Yessiree.

MINUTE

わ(ける)、わ(かる)、ブン、フン、ブ

ex. 一分 (いっぷん) - one minute
ex. 分かる (わかる) - to understand

ノ	八	分	分	

分

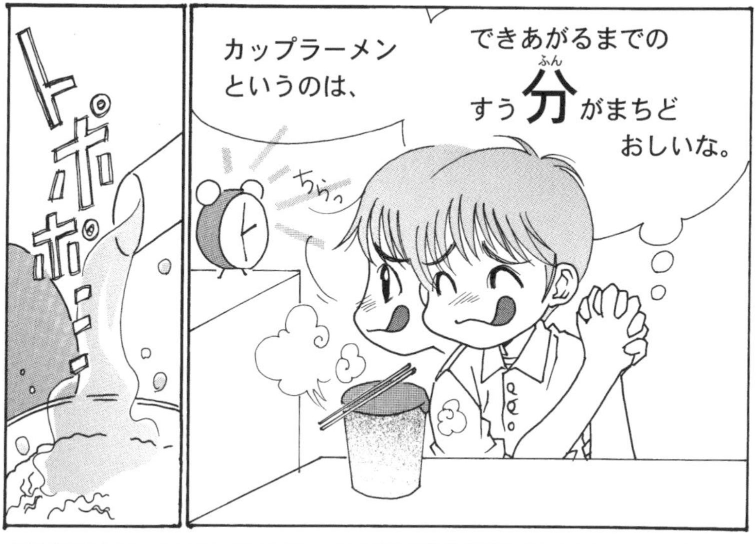

トポポ…
ちらっ
カップラーメンというのは、
できあがるまでのすう分(ふん)がまちどおしいな。

トポポ… (sound of water being poured)	*Boy:* カップラーメンというのは、できあがるまでのすう分がまちどおしいな。 It's those few minutes of anticipation while it cooks that make instant ramen taste so good!

時

TIME

とき、ジ

ex. 時計* (とけい) - watch, clock

ex. 一時 (いちじ) - one o'clock

もうこんな
時かん。
どうしようー。
いまなん時
だとおもって
いるの！？
おそくまで
あそんでばかり！
べんきょうも
しなさい！

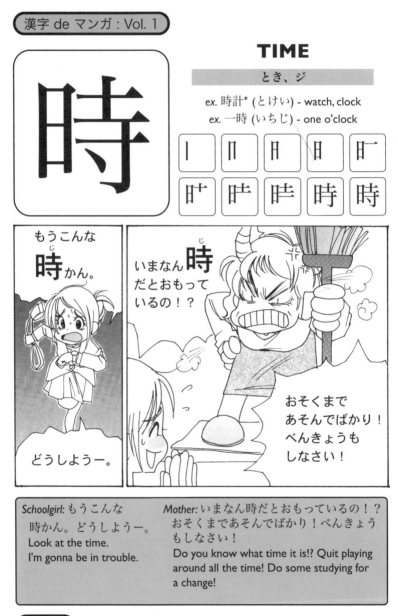

Schoolgirl: もうこんな時かん。どうしようー。
Look at the time.
I'm gonna be in trouble.

Mother: いまなん時だとおもっているの！？おそくまであそんでばかり！べんきょうもしなさい！
Do you know what time it is!? Quit playing around all the time! Do some studying for a change!

INTERVAL

あいだ、ま、カン、ケン

ex. 時間 (じかん) - time

ex. 中間 (ちゅうかん) - midway

ex. 人間 (にんげん) - human

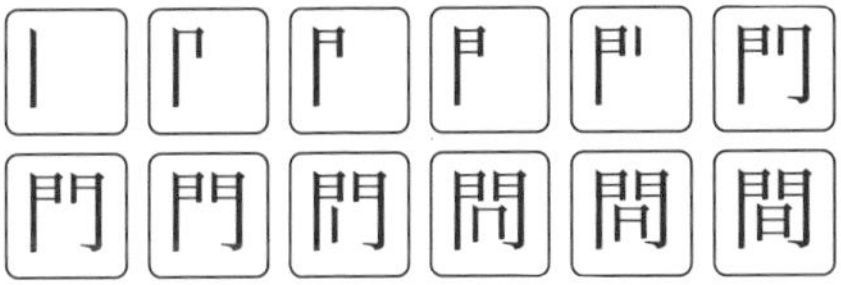

間

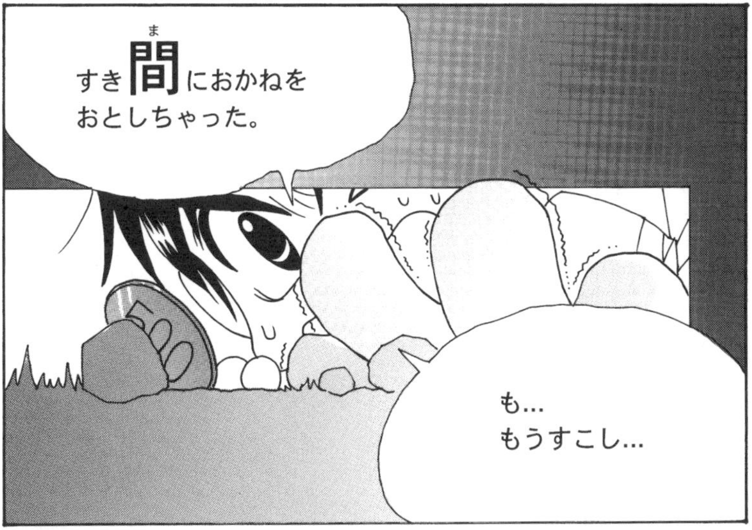
すき間(ま)におかねを
おとしちゃった。
も...
もうすこし...

Boy (reaching into a storm drain): すき間におかねを おとしちゃった。も...もうすこし...

My coin fell into this little space. Ju...just a little bit more...

年

YEAR

とし、ネン

ex. 今年 (ことし) - this year

ex. 去年* (きょねん) - last year

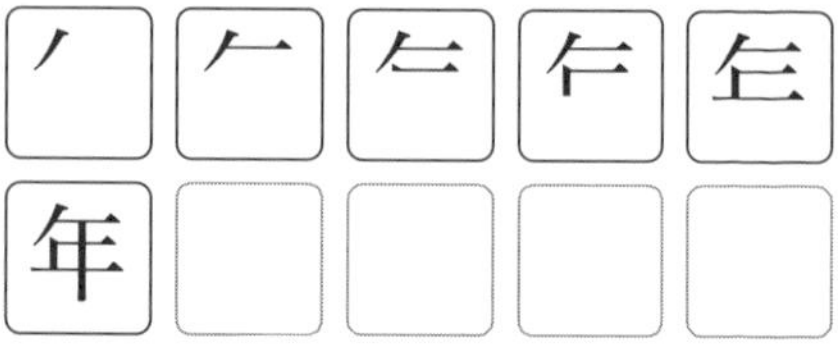

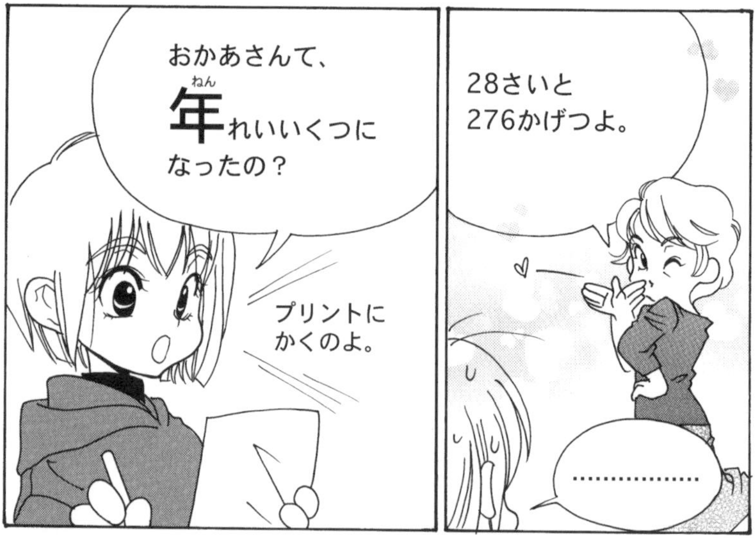

おかあさんて、
年(ねん)れいいくつに
なったの？
プリントに
かくのよ。
28さいと
276かげつよ。
……………….

Girl: おかあさんて、年れいいくつになったの？プリントにかくのよ。
Mom, how old will you be this year?
I need to put your age on this form.

Mother: 28さいと276かげつよ。
28 years and 276 months.

Girl: (speechless)

THIS / NOW

今

いま、コン

ex. 今日 (きょう) - this day; today

ex. 今月 (こんげつ) - this month

ノ 𠆢 亼 今

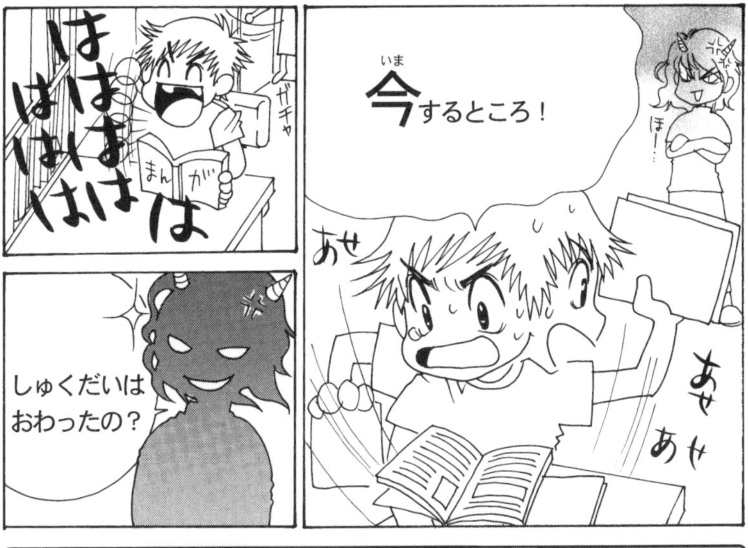
ははははははは
ガチャ
まんが
しゅくだいは
おわったの？
今(いま)するところ！
ほ！…
あせ
あせ
あせ

ははははははは
(boy laughing at comic book)

Mother: しゅくだいは おわったの？
Have you finished your homework?

Boy: 今するところ！
I was just about to start now!

あせ あせ あせ
(sound of quick movement)

毎

EVERY

マイ

ex. 毎日 (まいにち) - every day
ex. 毎月 (まいつき) - every month

ノ	𠂉	仁	𠃓	毎
毎				

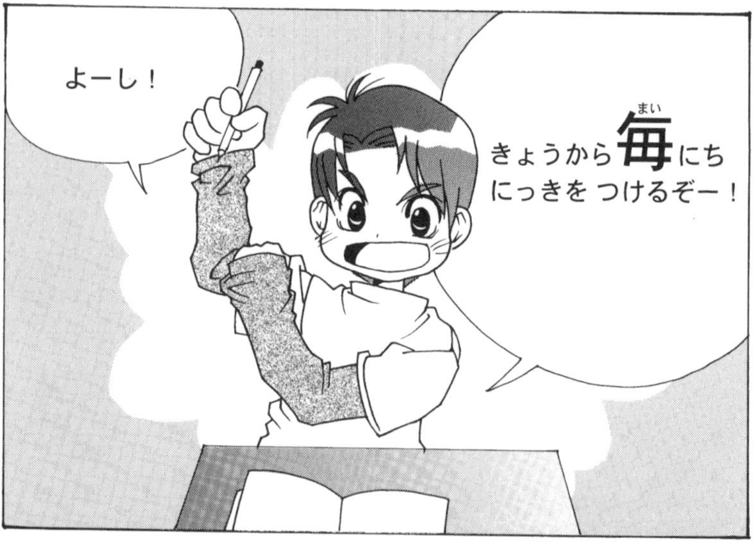
よーし！
きょうから毎(まい)にち
にっきを つけるぞー！

Student: よーし！きょうから
毎にちにっきをつけるぞー！
All right! Beginning today, I'm going
to keep a diary every day!

BEFORE

まえ、ゼン

ex. 五分前 (ごふんまえ) - five minutes ago
ex. 前日 (ぜんじつ) - the day before

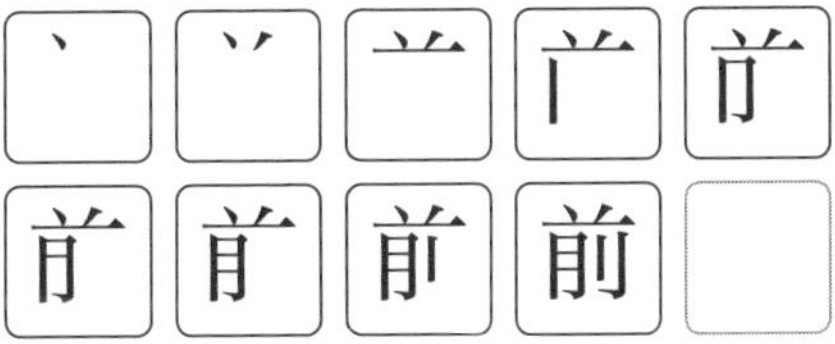

前

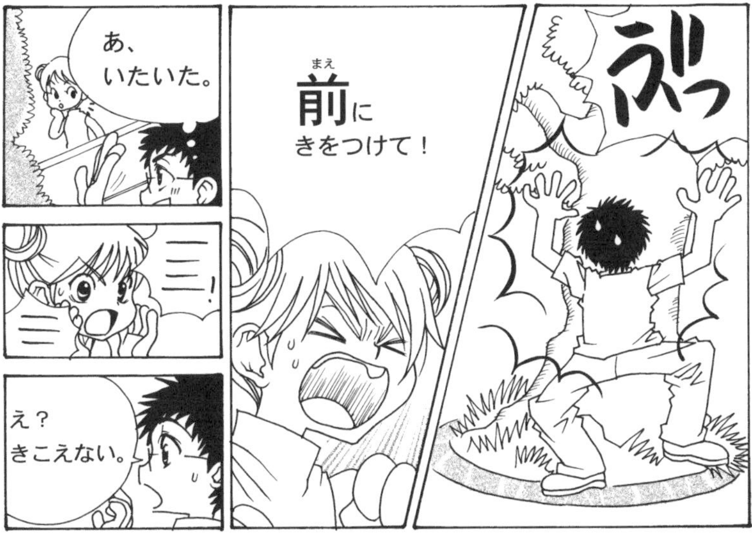
あ、いたいた。
！
え？きこえない。
前(まえ)にきをつけて！
ぶっ

Boy: あ、いたいた。
Ah, there she is!

Girl: —— *(inaudible)*!

Boy: え？きこえない。
What? I can't hear you.

Girl: 前にきをつけて！
Watch out in front of you!

ぶっ (thump)

午

NOON

ゴ

ex. 午前 (ごぜん) - a.m.

ex. 午後 (ごご) - p.m.

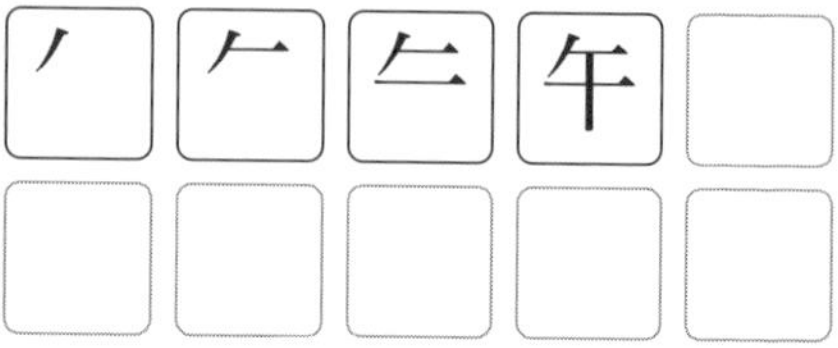

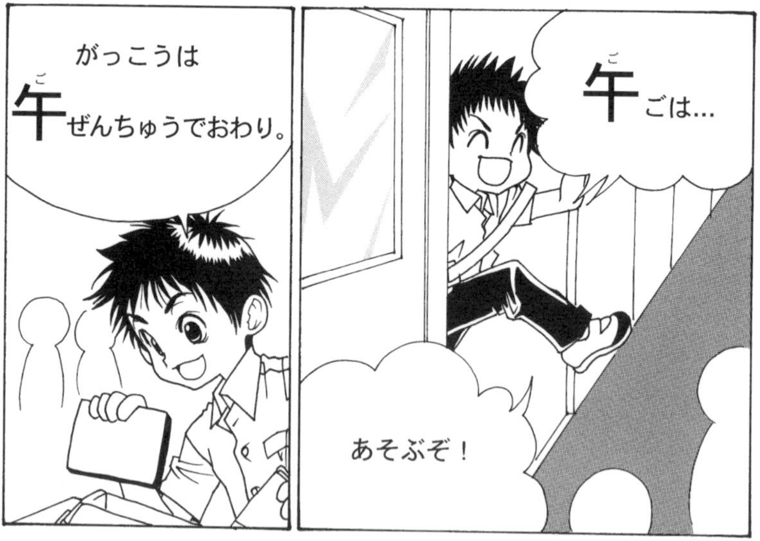
がっこうは 午(ご)ぜんちゅうでおわり。
午(ご)ごは…
あそぶぞ！

Schoolboy: がっこうは 午ぜんちゅうでおわり。
School ends at noon today.

午ごは…あそぶぞ！
This afternoon...I'm gonna have fun!

HALF

半

なか(ば)、ハン

ex. 一時半 (いちじはん) - 1:30

ex. 半年 (はんとし) - half a year

丶	丷	䒑	兰	半

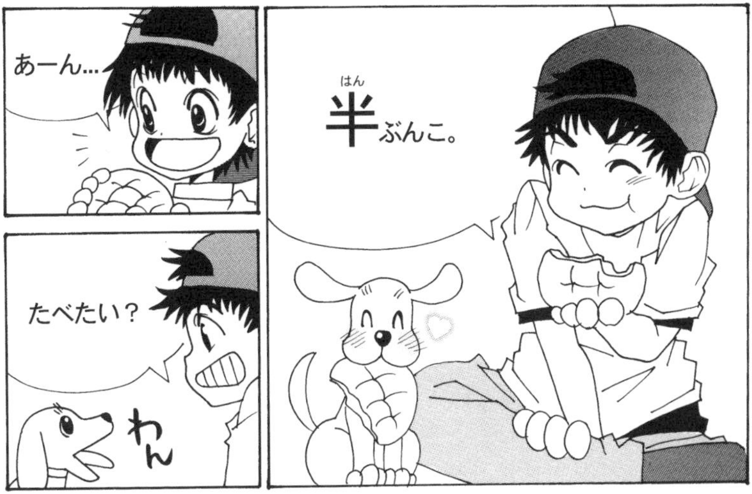
あーん…
たべたい？
わん
はん
半ぶんこ。

Boy: あーん…
Yum!

たべたい？
You want to eat some too?

わん (dog's "woof")

半ぶんこ。
OK, half each.

何

WHAT?

なに、なん

ex. 何時間 (なんじかん) - what time?

ex. 何人 (なんにん) - how many people?

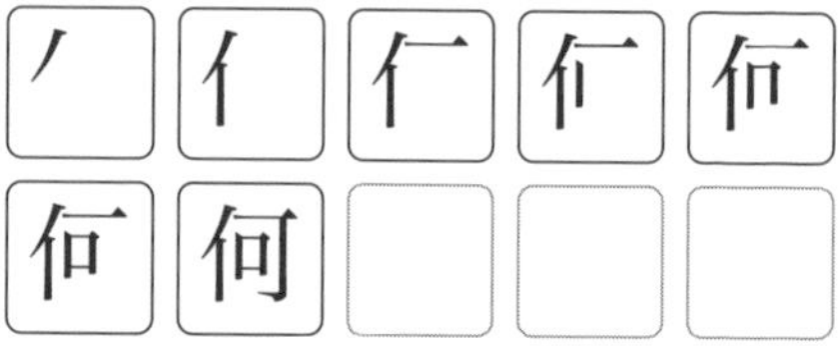

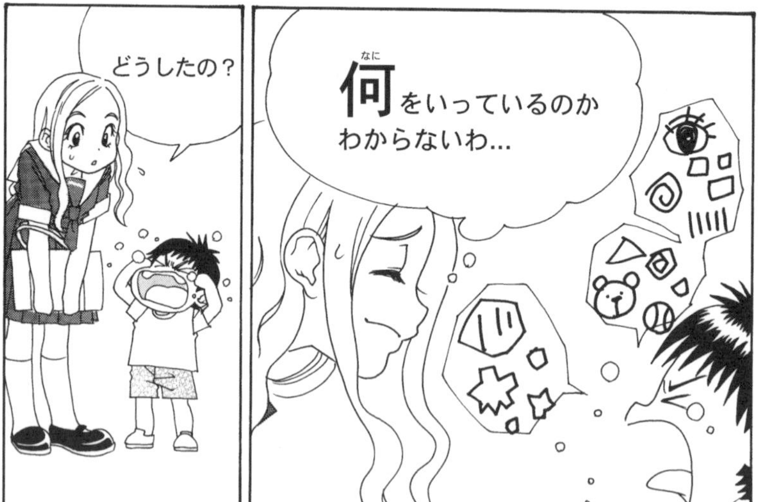
どうしたの？
何をいっているのか
わからないわ…

Sister: どうしたの？
What's wrong?

何をいっているのかわからないわ…
I have no idea what he's saying...

AFTER / BACK

のち、うし(ろ)、あと、ゴ、ゴウ

ex. 二日後 (ふつかご) - two days later
ex. 後ろ (うしろ) - behind

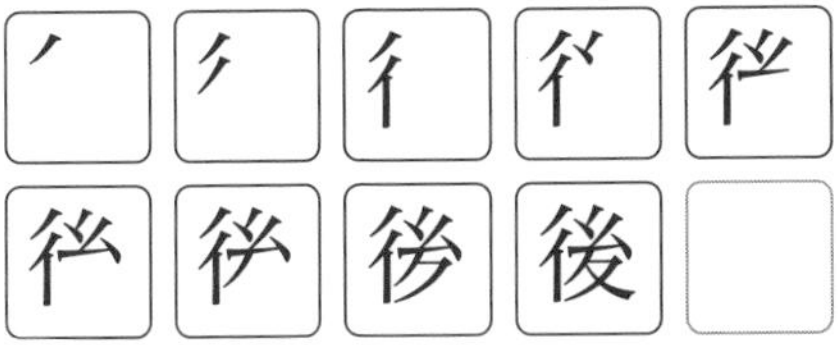

後

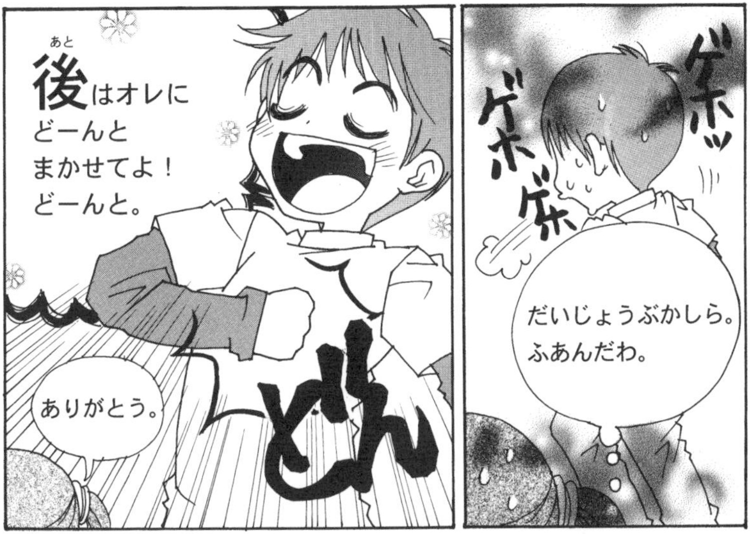
後(あと)はオレにどーんとまかせてよ！どーんと。
ありがとう。
どん
ゲホゲホゲホッ
だいじょうぶかしら。ふあんだわ。

Boy: 後はオレにどーんとまかせてよ！
どーんと。
Leave the rest up to me! I'll take care of it.

Girl: ありがとう。
Thanks.

どん (chest-thumping)

ゲホゲホゲホッ
(coughing)

Girl: だいじょうぶかしら。
ふあんだわ。
I hope things will be OK.
I'm a bit worried now.

先

AHEAD

さき、セン

ex. 先月 (せんげつ) - last month
ex. 先生 (せんせい) - teacher

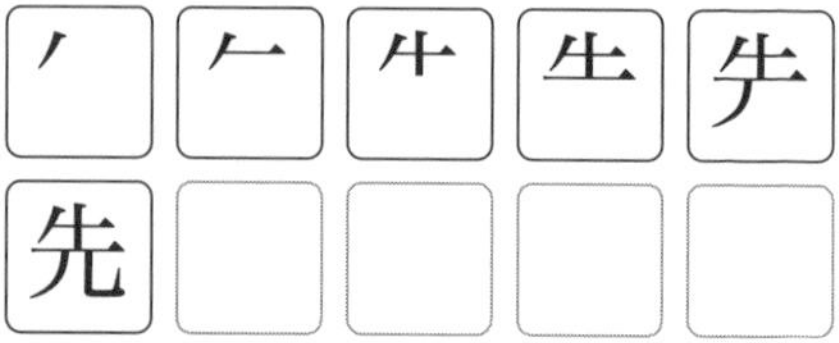

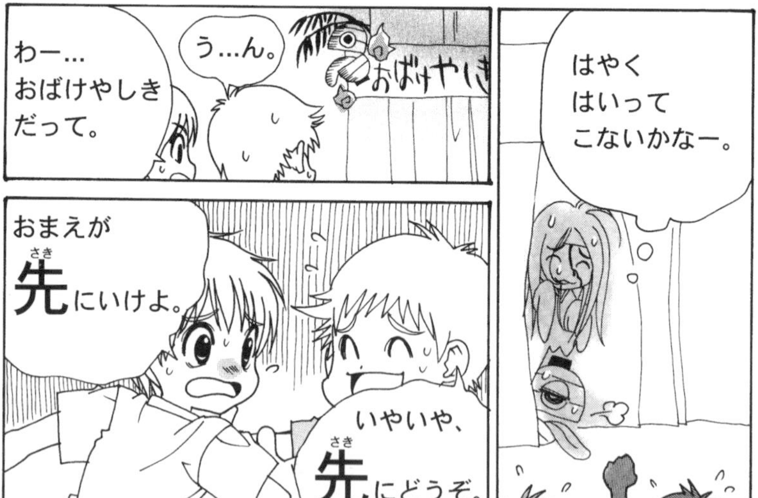
わー…
おばけやしき
だって。
う…ん。
おばけやしき
おまえが
先(さき)にいけよ。
いやいや、
先(さき)にどうぞ。
はやく
はいって
こないかなー。

First boy: わー… おばけやしきだって。
Hey, it's the haunted house.

Second boy: う…ん。 Yeah.

First boy: おまえが先にいけよ。 You go first.

Second boy: いやいや、先にどうぞ。 Nah, that's all right. You go first.

Witch: はやくはいって こないかなー。
I wish they'd hurry up and come inside!

HIGH / EXPENSIVE

たか、たか(い)、コウ

ex. 高すぎる (たかすぎる) - too expensive
ex. 高校 (こうこう) - high school

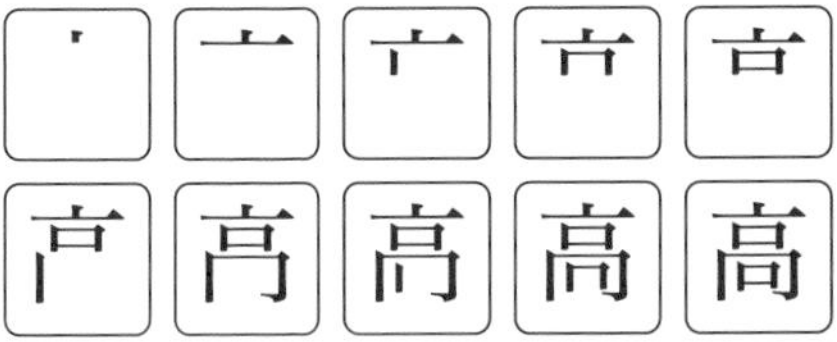

高

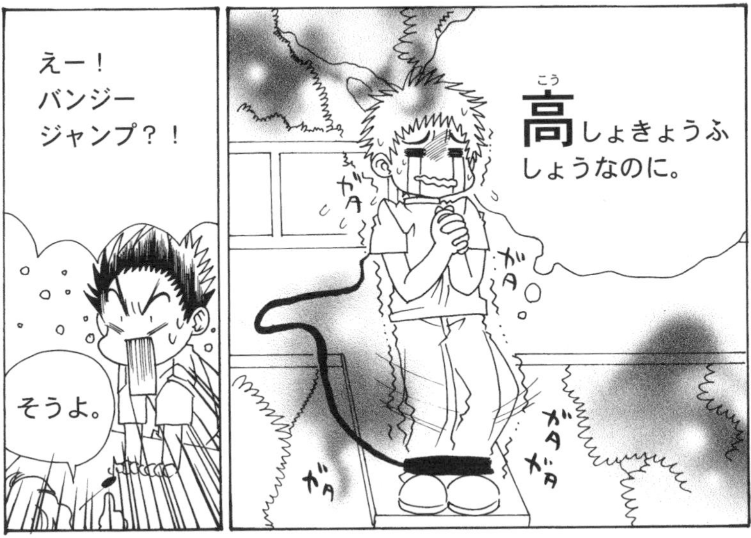
えー！
バンジー
ジャンプ？！
そうよ。
こう
高しょきょうふしょうなのに。
ガタ
ガタ
ガタ
ガタ
ガタ

First boy: えー！
バンジージャンプ？！
Huh? You're gonna bungee-jump?!

Second boy: そうよ。
That's right.

Second boy: 高しょきょうふしょうなのに。
But I'm terrified of high places!

ガタ ガタ ガタ
(sound of knees knocking)

北

NORTH

きた、ホク

ex. 北口* (きたぐち) - north entrance

ex. 北米* (ほくべい) - North America

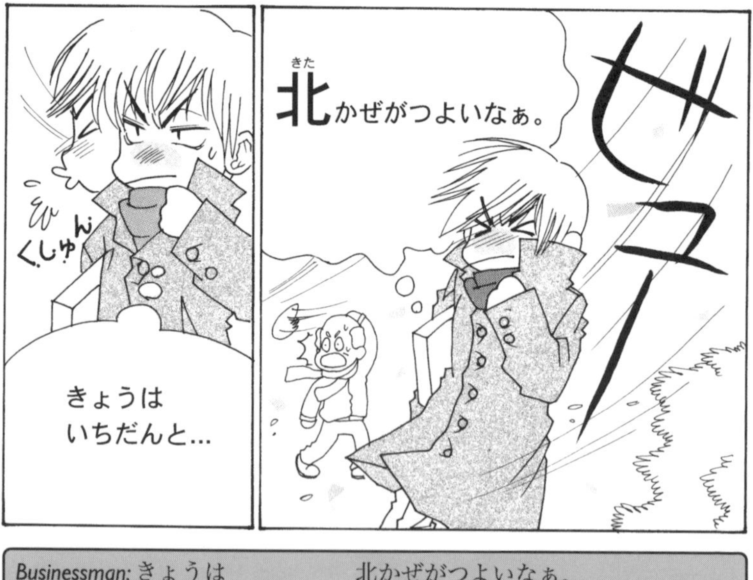
くしゅん
きょうは
いちだんと…
北かぜがつよいなぁ。
ビュー

Businessman: きょうは いちだんと…

Today in particular...

くしゅん

(sound of sneezing)

北かぜがつよいなぁ。

...the wind from the north is strong.

ビュー

(sound of a strong wind)

SOUTH

みなみ、ナン

ex. 南口* (みなみぐち) - south entrance
ex. 南米* (なんべい) - South America

一	十	广	冇	冇
冇	声	南	南	

南

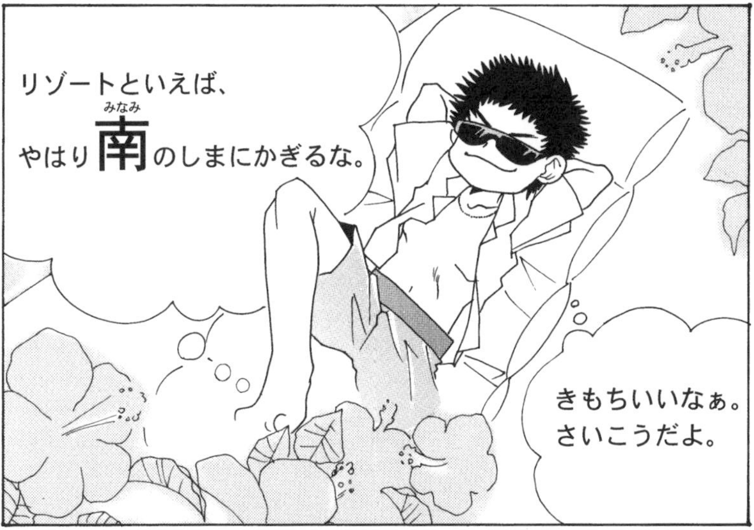
リゾートといえば、
やはり南(みなみ)のしまにかぎるな。
きもちいいなぁ。
さいこうだよ。

Sunbather: リゾートといえば、やはり南のしまにかぎるな。
When you think of a paradise resort, it's gotta be on an island in the south.
きもちいいなぁ。さいこうだよ。
I feel great. It's beautiful.

東

EAST

ひがし、トウ

ex. 東口* (ひがしぐち) - east entrance

ex. 東京* (とうきょう) - Tokyo

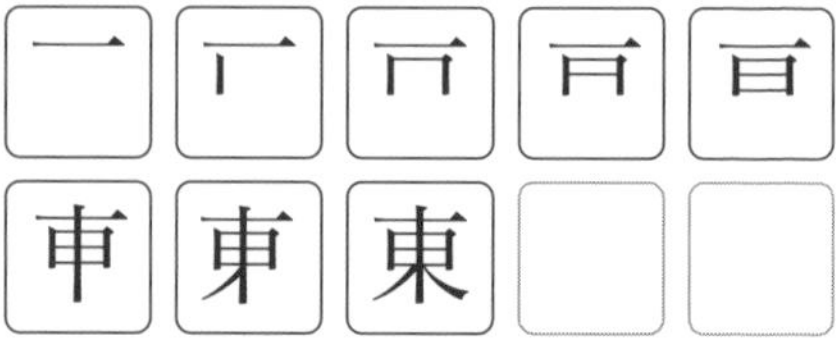

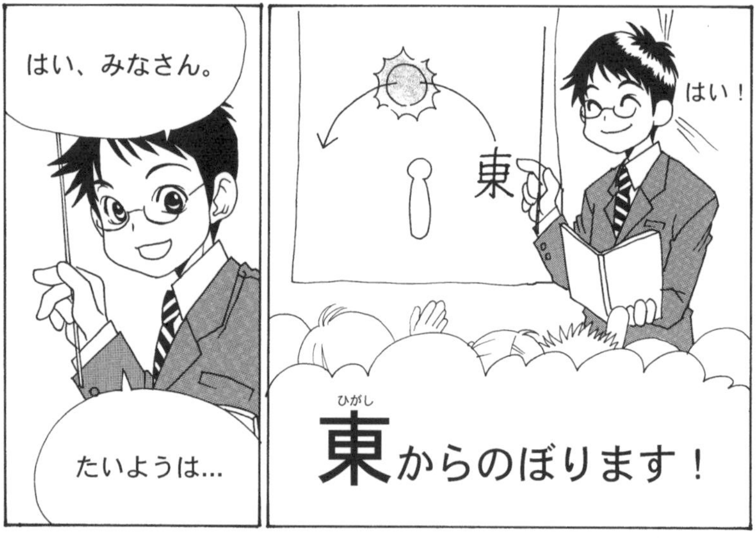
はい、みなさん。
たいようは…
東
はい！
ひがし
東からのぼります！

Teacher: はい、みなさん。
たいようは…
OK, everyone. The sun...

Students (in unison): 東からのぼります！
Rises from the east!

Teacher: はい！
That's correct!

WEST

にし、セイ、サイ

ex. 西口* (にしぐち) - west entrance
ex. 西洋* (せいよう) - Western countries

西

………
わっ、
はんぶんだけ ひやけしてる？！
西びばかりあびて
このとおりさ。
なるほど。

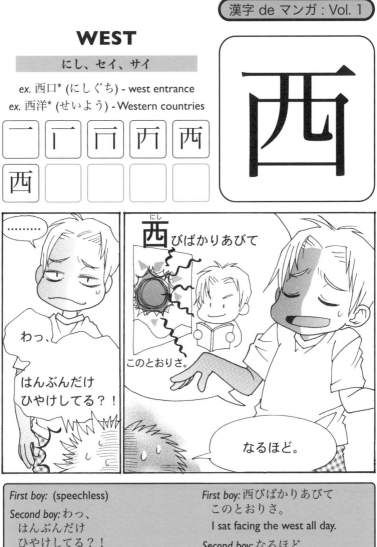

First boy: (speechless)

Second boy: わっ、
はんぶんだけ
ひやけしてる？！
Yikes! Why are you sunburned on just one side of your body?!

First boy: 西びばかりあびて
このとおりさ。
I sat facing the west all day.

Second boy: なるほど。
That explains it.

上

UP / ABOVE

うえ、あ(げ)る、あ(が)る、ジョウ

ex. 年上 (としうえ) - elder

ex. 上下 (じょうげ) - up and down

丨 ⺊ 上

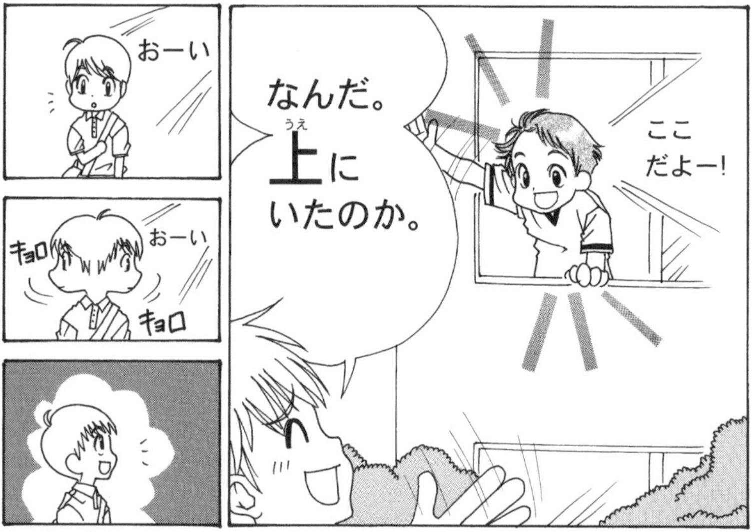
おーい
キョロ
おーい
キョロ
ここだよー!
なんだ。上(うえ)にいたのか。

Big brother: おーい
Hey!

キョロ キョロ
(sound of head turning left and right)

Little brother: ここだよー。
Here I am.

Big brother: なんだ。上にいたのか。
Oh, you're up there!

DOWN / UNDER

下

した、くだ、さ(げ)る、カ、ゲ

ex. 年下 (としした) - junior

ex. 下さい (ください) - please

一	丅	下		

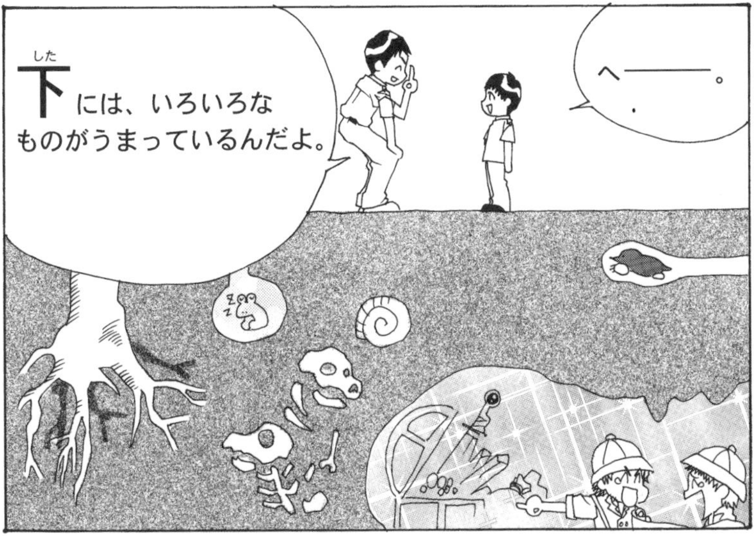
下(した)には、いろいろなものがうまっているんだよ。
へ——。

Big boy: 下には、いろいろなものがうまっているんだよ。
There are many things buried under the ground.

Little boy: へー。
Really?

左

LEFT

ひだり、サ

ex. 左側* (ひだりがわ) - left-hand side

ex. 左右 (さゆう) - either side

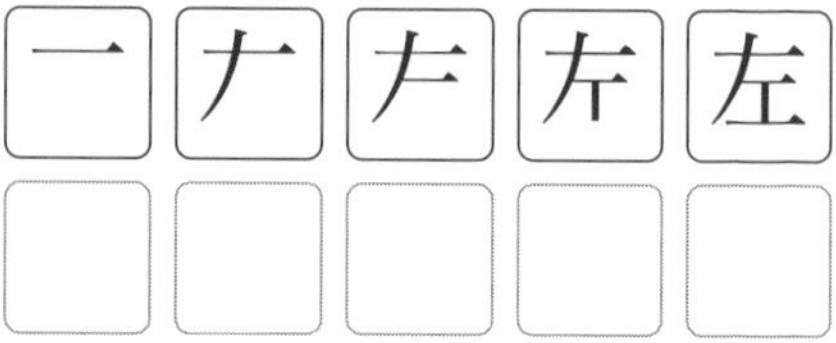

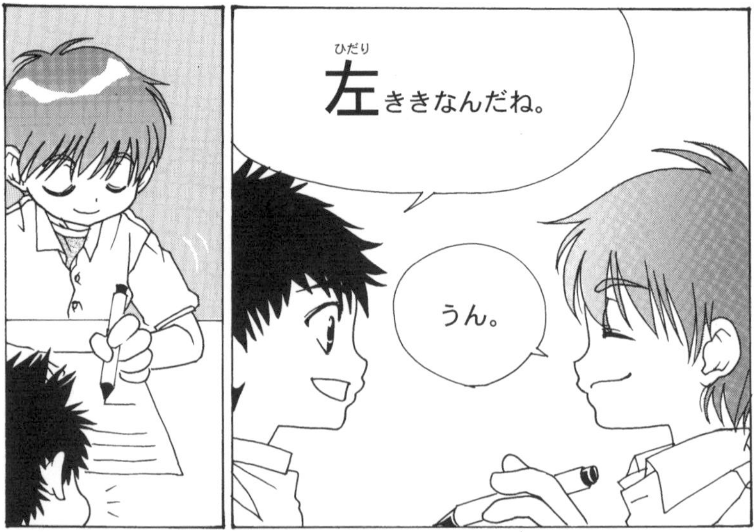
左(ひだり)ききなんだね。
うん。

First boy: 左ききなんだね。

So, you're a lefty.

Second boy: うん。

Yep.

RIGHT

右

みぎ、ウ、ユウ

ex. 右側* (みぎがわ) - right-hand side
ex. 右巻* (みぎまき) - clockwise

ノ ナ 𠂇 右 右

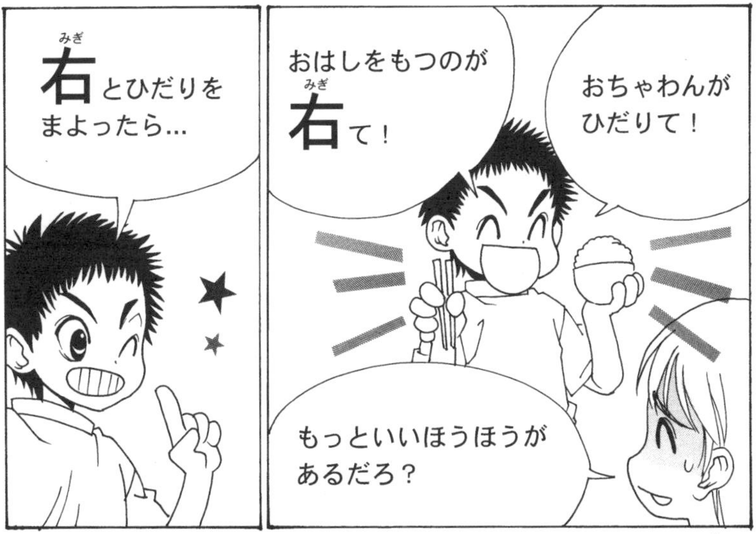
右（みぎ）とひだりを
まよったら…
おはしをもつのが
右（みぎ）て！
おちゃわんが
ひだりて！
もっといいほうほうが
あるだろ？

Boy: 右とひだりを
まよったら…
If you're not sure which is left and which is right...

Boy: おはしをもつのが右て！
おちゃわんがひだりて！
You hold chopsticks in your right hand!
And the rice bowl in your left hand!

Girl: もっといいほうほうがあるだろ？
Isn't there a better way to remember?

来

COME

く(る)、ライ

ex. 来月 (らいげつ) - next month

ex. 来年 (らいねん) - next year

一 丆 フ 立 平 来 来

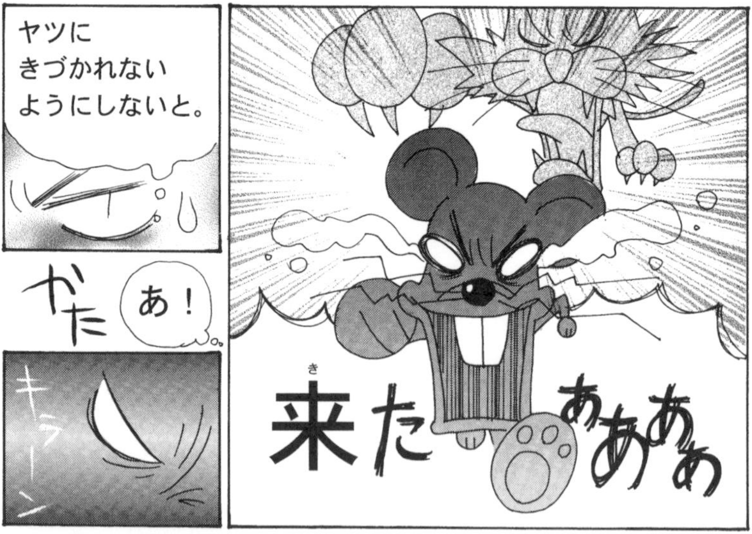

ヤツに きづかれない ようにしないと。
かた
あ！
キラーン
来たああああ

Mouse: ヤツにきづかれないようにしないと。
I can't let him see me.

かた (strange noise)

あ！ Uh-oh!

キラーン (glint of cat's eye)

Mouse: 来たああああ
Here he comes!

GO

行

い(く)、おこな(う)、コウ、ギョウ

ex. 行く (いく) - to go

ex. 旅行* (りょこう) - travel

行

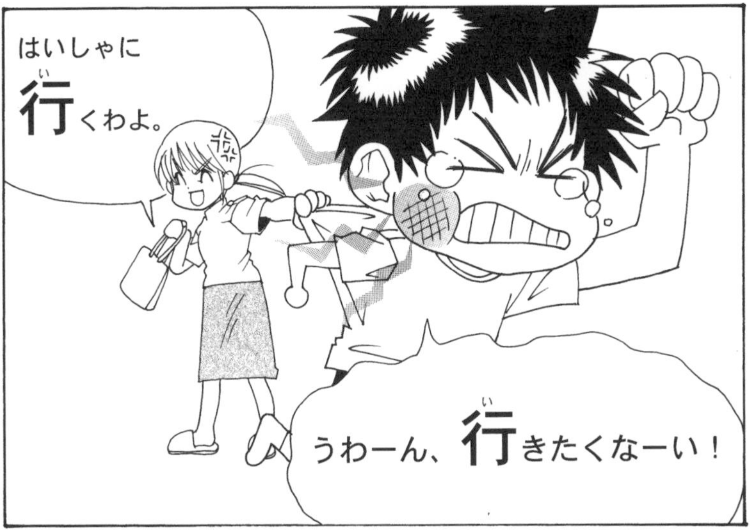
はいしゃに行くわよ。
うわーん、行きたくなーい！

Mother: はいしゃに行くわよ。

We're going to the dentist.

Boy: うわーん、行きたくなーい！

Waaahh! I don't want to go!

入

ENTER / PUT IN

い(る)、い(れる)、はい(る)、ニュウ

ex. 入口* (いりぐち) - entrance

ex. 入学 (にゅうがく) - matriculation

ノ 入

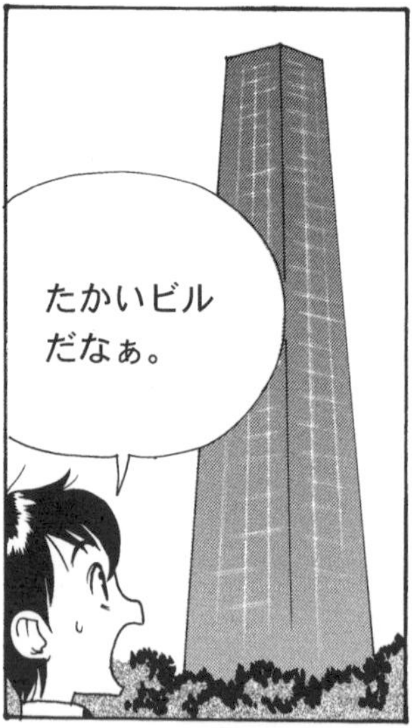
たかいビル
だなぁ。

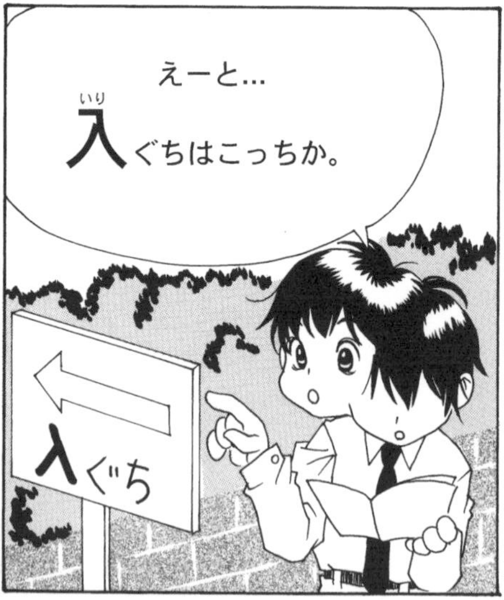
えーと…
入(いり)ぐちはこっちか。
入ぐち

Businessman: たかいビル
だなぁ。
That sure is a tall building.

えーと… 入ぐちはこっちか。
Let's see...The entrance is this way.

入ぐち ("Entrance" sign)

LEAVE / TAKE OUT

で(る)、だ(す)、シュツ

ex. 出口* (でぐち) - exit
ex. 出前 (でまえ) - home-delivered food

丨	屮	中	出	出

このへん
オバケが
出そう...

出たぁ！

出るほうが
おどろいたよ。
にんげんこわい。

Frightened girl: この
へんオバケが
出そう...
I'm sure ghosts
come out
around here...

Frightened girl: 出たぁ！
They're on the loose!

キャー (breathless scream)
ちゅー (squeak of mouse)
ビクッ (sound of surprise)
ドキドキ (heavy heartbeats)

Ghost: 出るほうが
おどろいたよ。
にんげんこわい。
I'm supposed to do
the haunting, but
humans scare me!

REST

やす(む)、やす(まる)、キュウ

ex. 夏休み (なつやすみ) - summer vacation
ex. 休日 (きゅうじつ) - holiday; day off

はあ はあ	ぜーはー
(heavy panting)	(slower panting)

Hiker: ちょっと休けい。
　　Time to rest.

OUTSIDE

そと、ほか、はず(す)、ガイ

ex. 外国人 (がいこくじん) - foreigner
ex. 外食 (がいしょく) - eating out

ノ	ク	タ	タ|	外

外

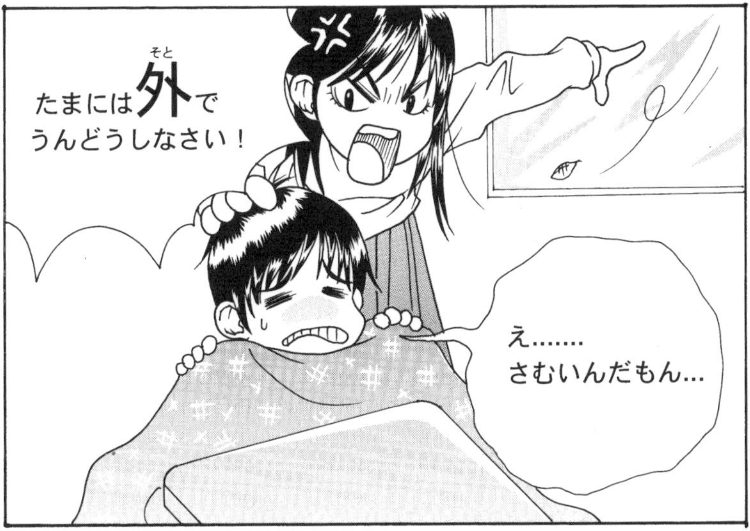
たまには外でうんどうしなさい！
え.......
さむいんだもん...

Mother: たまには外でうんどうしなさい！
You need to go outside and get some exercise!

Boy: え…　さむいんだもん…
(Whining) But it's so cold...

小

SMALL

ちい(さい)、こ、お、ショウ

ex. 小雨 (こさめ) - light rain (drizzle)
ex. 小学校 (しょうがっこう) - primary school

亅	小	小		

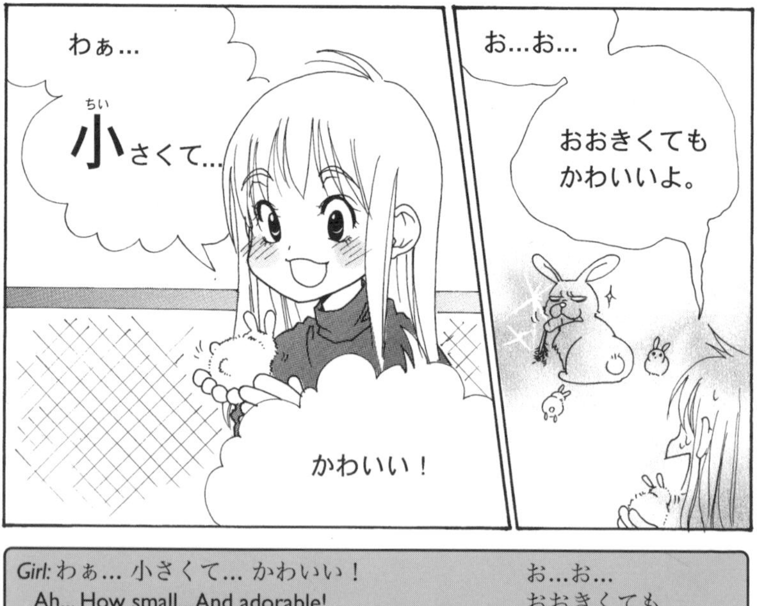

わぁ…
小(ちい)さくて…
かわいい！
お…お…
おおきくても
かわいいよ。

Girl: わぁ… 小さくて… かわいい！
Ah... How small...And adorable!

お…お…
おおきくても
かわいいよ。
Oh, of course, the big ones are cute too.

MIDDLE / IN

なか、チュウ

ex. 中学校 (ちゅうがっこう) - middle school
ex. 中国 (ちゅうごく) - China

丨	冂	口	中

Boy: このハコの中って
なにかな？
I wonder what's in this box?

わーっ！
Yikes!

ビョョョ
(boing)

大

BIG

おお、おお(きい)、ダイ、タイ

ex. 大人 (おとな) - adult
ex. 大学 (だいがく) - university

一	ナ	大		

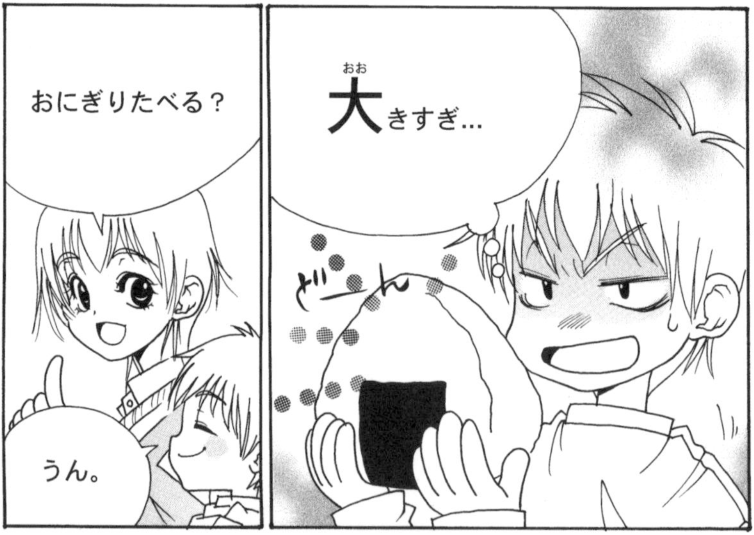
おにぎりたべる？
うん。
大(おお)きすぎ…
どーん

Mother: おにぎりたべる？
Do you want to eat a rice ball?

Boy: うん。
Please!

Boy: 大きすぎ…
It's too big...

どーん
(sound of surprise, similar to "gong")

CHIEF / LONG

なが(い)、チョウ

ex. 校長 (こうちょう) - school principal
ex. 長男 (ちょうなん) - eldest son

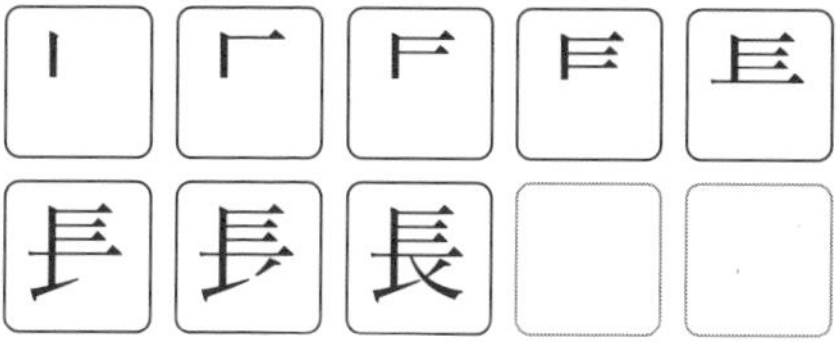

長

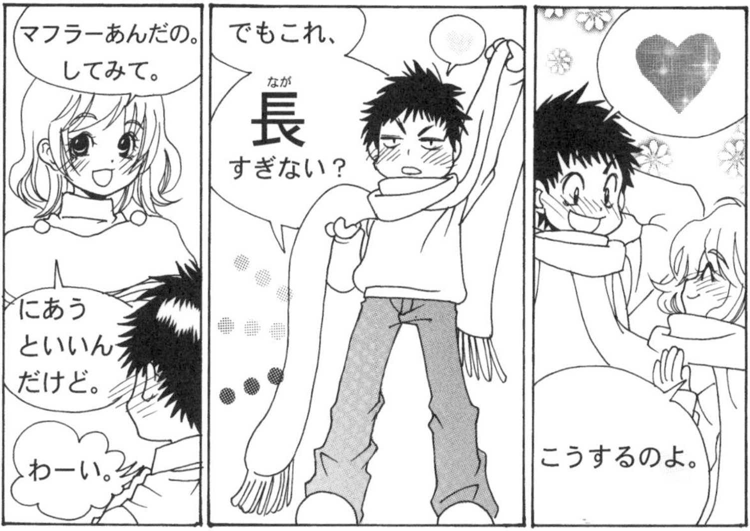

マフラーあんだの。してみて。
にあうといいんだけど。
わーい。
でもこれ、
長すぎない？
こうするのよ。

Girl: マフラーあんだの。してみて。にあうといいんだけど。
I knitted a muffler. Try it on. I hope you like it.

Boy: わーい。
Thanks!

Boy: でもこれ、長すぎない？
But isn't it too long?

Girl: こうするのよ。
This is how we wear it.

MAN

おとこ、ダン、ナン

ex. 男の人 (おとこのひと) - man
ex. 男の子 (おとこのこ) - boy

Girl:	男なんだから、なんとか しなさいよ！	Boy:	こわいものはこわいんだよー！ わー！
	You're a boy, do something!		He's so scary! Yikes!
Boy:	そんなこといったって...		ガルルル
	Yeah, but...		(dog's growl)

WOMAN

おんな、ジョ

ex. 女の人 (おんなのひと) - woman
ex. 女の子 (おんなのこ) - girl

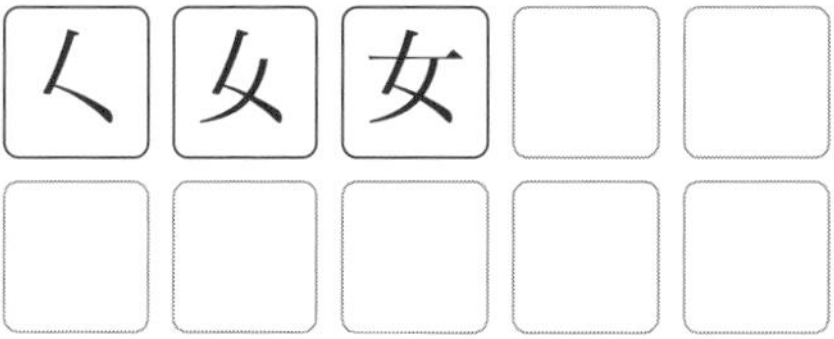

女

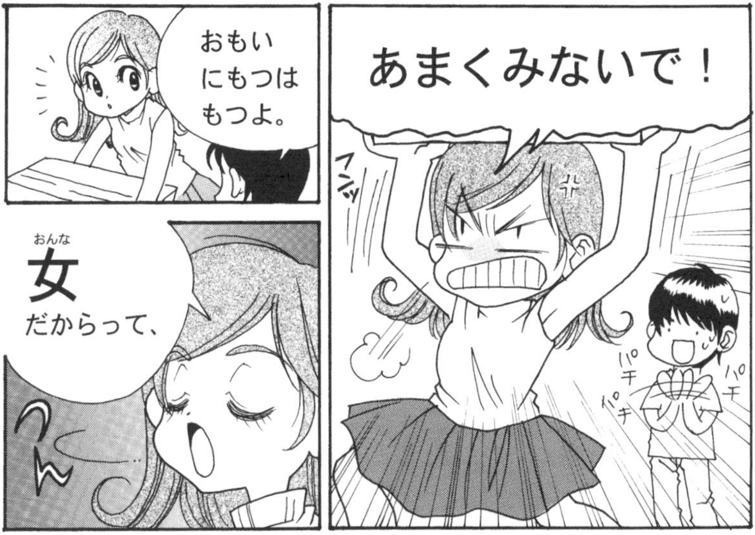
おもいにもつはもつよ。
おんな
女
だからって、
つん
あまくみないで！
フンッ
パチ
パチ
パチ

Boy: おもいにもつはもつよ。
I'll carry the heavy ones!

Girl: 女だからって、
Just because I'm a girl...

つん (humph)

Girl: あまくみないで！
...doesn't mean I'm weak and helpless!

フンッ (oomph)

パチパチパチ (clapping)

父

FATHER

ちち、フ

ex. お父さん (おとうさん) - father (polite)

ex. 父母 (ふぼ) - parents

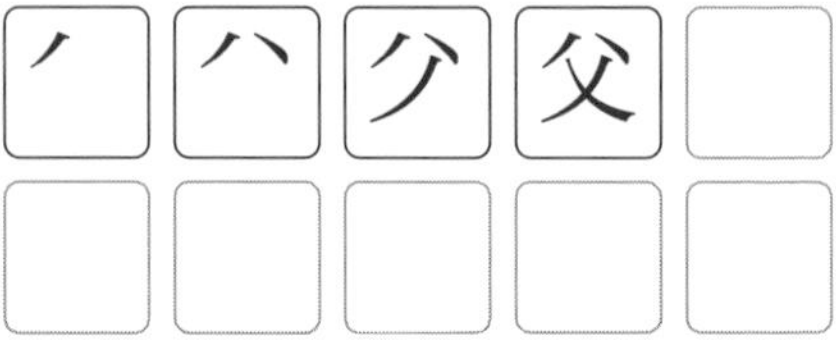

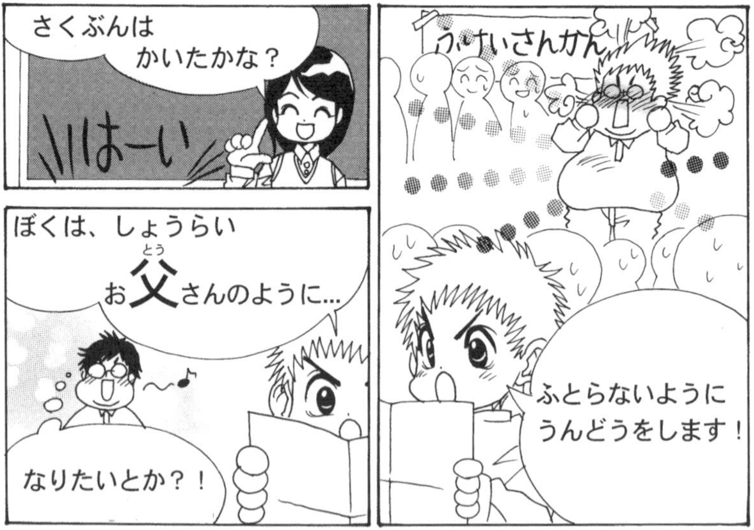
さくぶんは かいたかな？
はーい
ぼくは、しょうらい お父(とう)さんのように...
なりたいとか？！
ふけいさんかん
ふとらないように うんどうをします！

Teacher: さくぶんはかいたかな？ Did everyone finish their essays?

Students (in unison): はーい Yes!

Boy (reading essay): ぼくは、しょうらい お父さんのように... "My Father": When I grow up...

Father (listening): なりたいとか？！ He wants to be like me?!

ふけいさんかん(び) ("Parents Day" sign)

Boy (still reading): ふとらないように うんどうをします！ I'll exercise so I won't be fat like him!

MOTHER

はは、ボ

ex. お母さん (おかあさん) - mother (polite)
ex. 母国語 (ぼこくご) - mother tongue

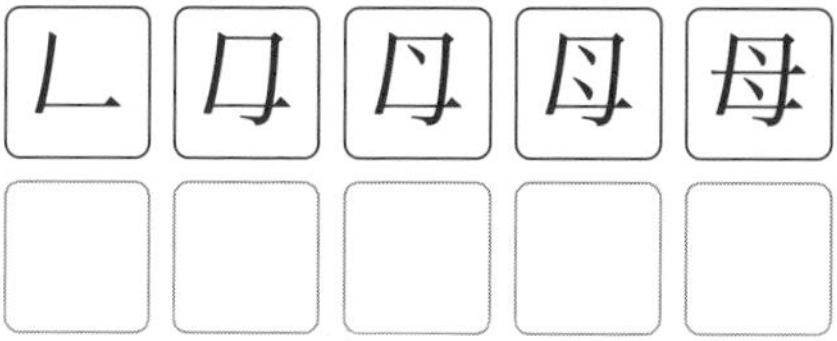

母

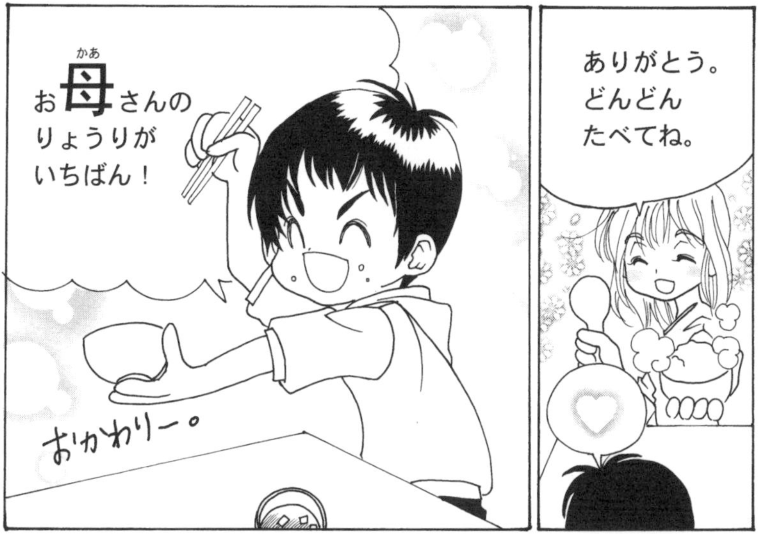
お母(かあ)さんのりょうりがいちばん！
おかわりー。
ありがとう。どんどんたべてね。

Boy: お母さんのりょうりがいちばん！
おかわりー。
Mom, your cooking is the best!
Some more, please!

Mother: ありがとう。
どんどんたべてね.
Thank you! Eat up!

人

PERSON

ひと、ジン、ニン

ex. 一人 (ひとり) - one person; alone
ex. 日本人 (にほんじん) - Japanese (people)

ノ	人			

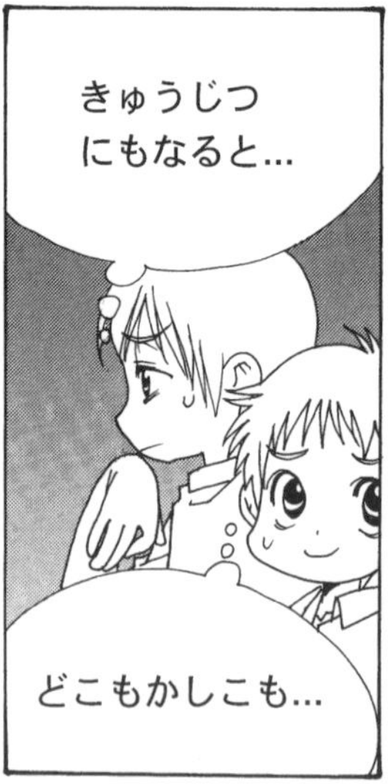
きゅうじつ
にもなると…
どこもかしこも…

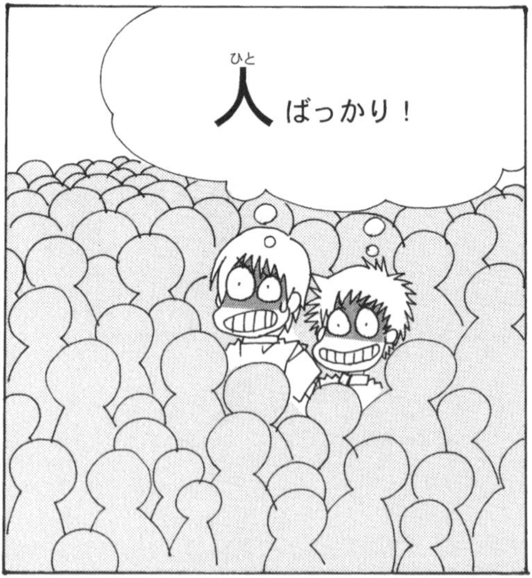
ひと
人ばっかり！

First boy: きゅうじつ
にもなると…
Come the weekend...

Second boy: どこもかしこも…
No matter which way you turn...

Both boys: 人ばっかり！
People are everywhere!

CHILD

こ、ご、シ、ス

ex. 子供たち* (こどもたち) - children
ex. 子守* (こもり) - babysitter

乛	了	子		

子

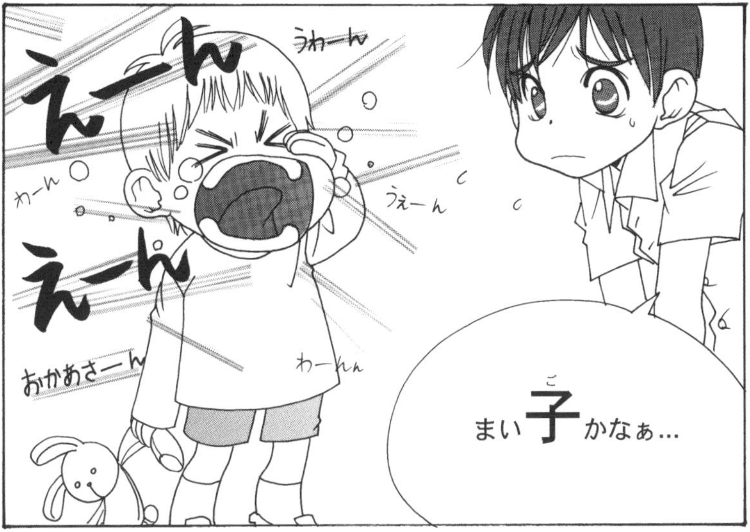
えーん
うわーん
わーん
うえーん
えーん
おかあさーん
わーんん
まい子かなぁ…

Toddler: えーん　えーん
おかあさーん…
(crying) Mommy!

Boy: まい子かなぁ…
A lost child?

友

FRIEND

とも、ユウ

ex. 友だち (ともだち) - friend(s)
ex. 学友 (がくゆう) - classmate

一	ナ	方	友	

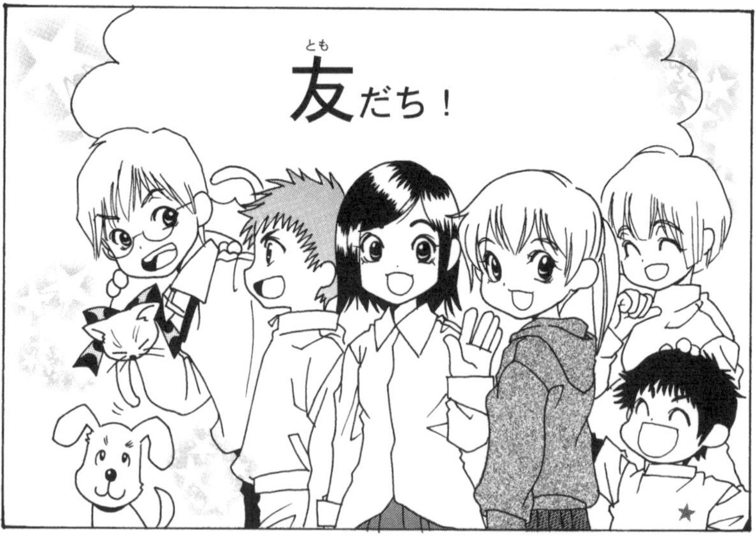
友だち！

Children (in unison): 友だち！
Friends!

LIFE / RAW

い(きる)、う(まれる)、セイ、ショウ

ex. 生まれる (うまれる) - to be born
ex. 人生 (じんせい) - life

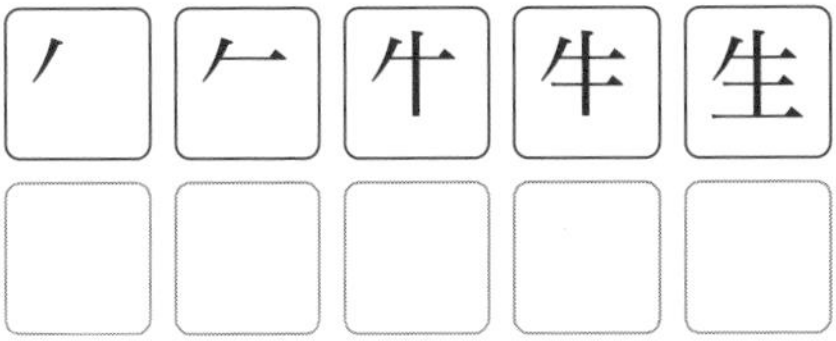

生

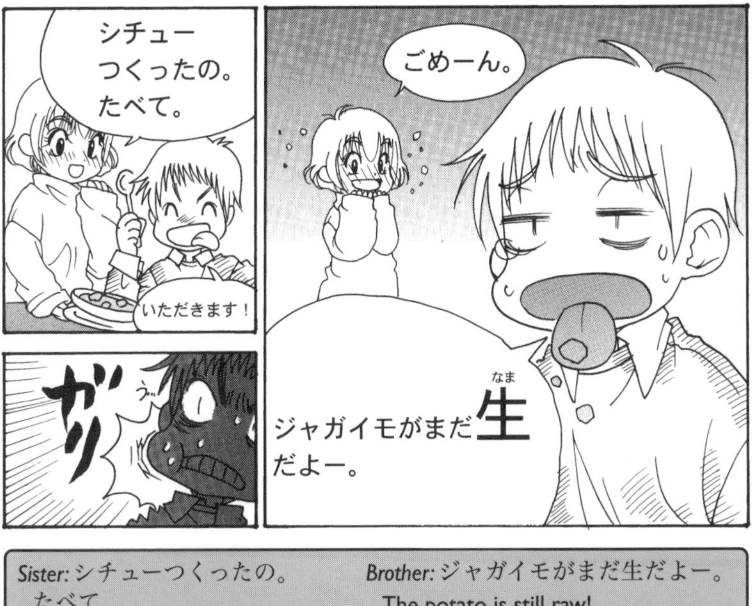

シチュー
つくったの。
たべて。
いただきます！
ガリ
う…
ごめーん。
ジャガイモがまだ生(なま)
だよー。

Sister: シチューつくったの。
たべて。
I made stew. Eat up!

Brother: いただきます！
Thanks!

ガリ (sound of shock)

Brother: ジャガイモがまだ生だよー。
The potato is still raw!

Sister: ごめーん。
Sorry.

山

MOUNTAIN

やま、サン

ex. 富士山* (ふじさん) - Mt. Fuji
ex. 火山 (かざん) - volcano

丨	山	山		

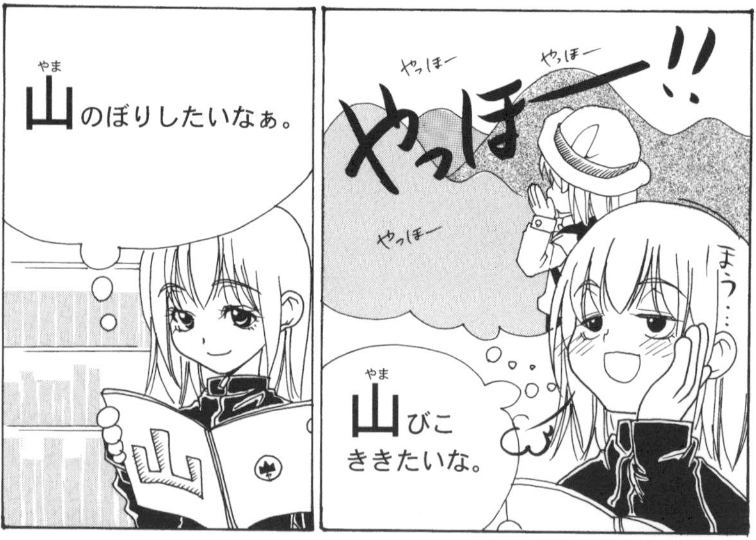
やま
山のぼりしたいなぁ。
やっほー
やっほー
やっほー!!
やっほー
ほう…
やま
山びこ
ききたいな。

Girl: 山のぼりしたいなぁ。
I'd love to go mountain-climbing.

やっほー！
(Sound of yodeling)
山びこききたいな。
Then I can hear the echo of my voice in the mountains!

RIVER

かわ、がわ、セン

ex. 小川 (おがわ) - small river (stream)
ex. 川下 (かわしも) - downstream

丿	川	川		

川

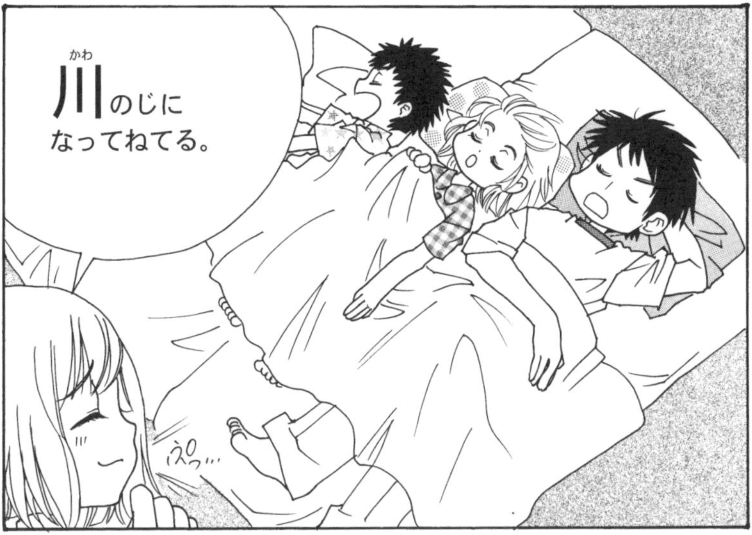
川(かわ)のじに
なってねてる。
ぷっ…

Mother: 川のじになってねてる。
They're sleeping side-by-side.

In Japan, it is common for children and parents to sleep together. When three family members (usually the mother one on side, father on the other and a small child in the middle, are lying next to one another, the formation resembles the kanji character for river (川) and is thus called a kawa-no-ji ("kanji for river").

天

HEAVEN / SKY

あま、あめ、テン

ex. 天気 (てんき) - weather

ex. 雨天 (うてん) - rainy weather

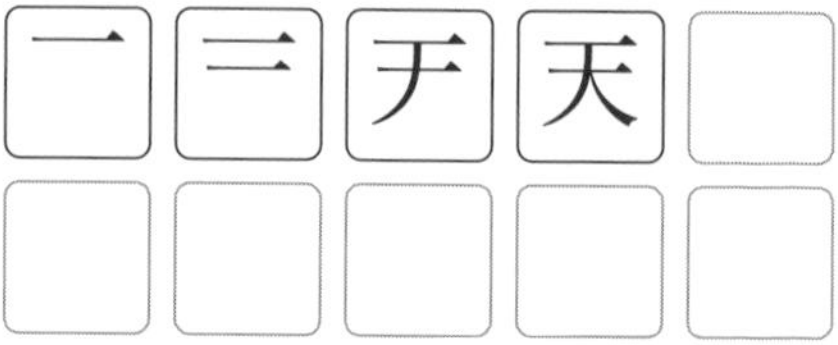

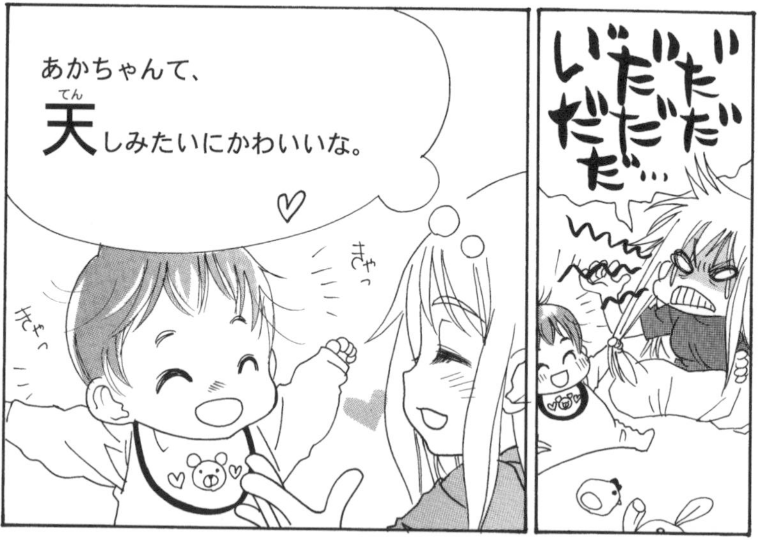
あかちゃんて、
てん
天しみたいにかわいいな。
きゃっ
きゃっ
いだだだだだだ…

Girl: あかちゃんて、天しみたいにかわいいな。
Babies are as cute as angels!

きゃっ　きゃっ
(Sound of baby cooing)

Girl: いだだだだだ！
Eeeooowww!

SPIRIT / GAS

気

キ、ケ

ex. 電気 (でんき) - electricity

ex. 気分 (きぶん) - feeling; mood

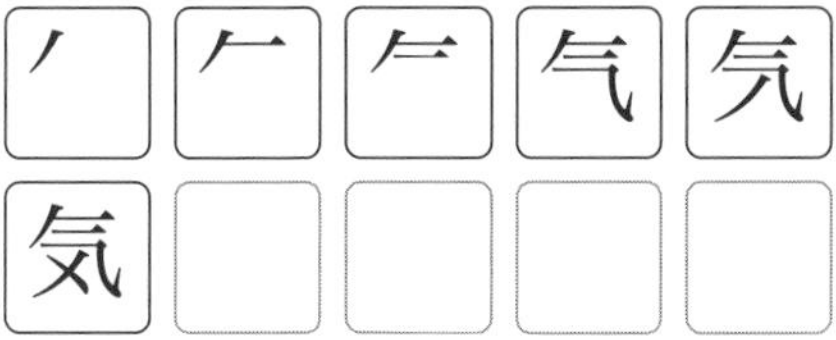

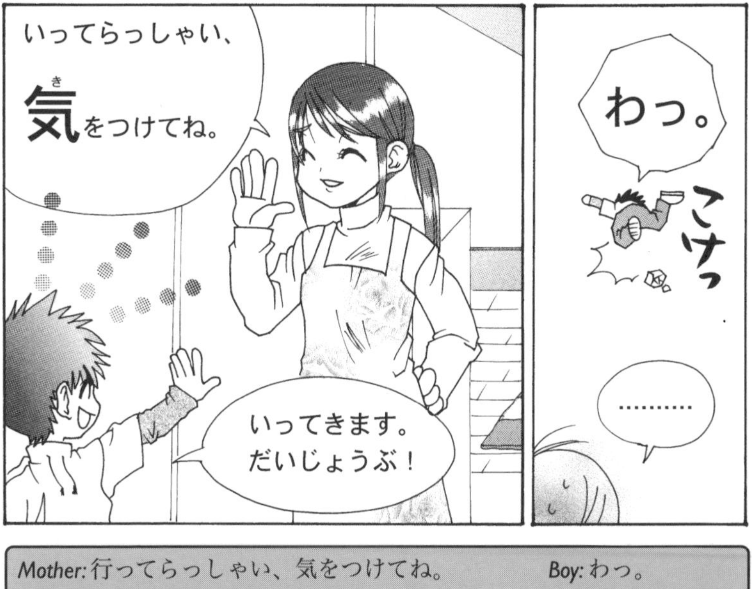
いってらっしゃい、
気をつけてね。
いってきます。
だいじょうぶ！
わっ。
こけっ
....

Mother: 行ってらっしゃい、気をつけてね。
See you later! Be careful now!

Boy: いってきます。だいじょうぶ！
See ya. I'll be fine!

Boy: わっ。
Oops.

こけっ
(tripping noise)

Mother: (speechless)

雨

RAIN

あめ、あま、ウ

ex. 大雨 (おおあめ) - heavy rain
ex. 雨水 (あまみず) - rainwater

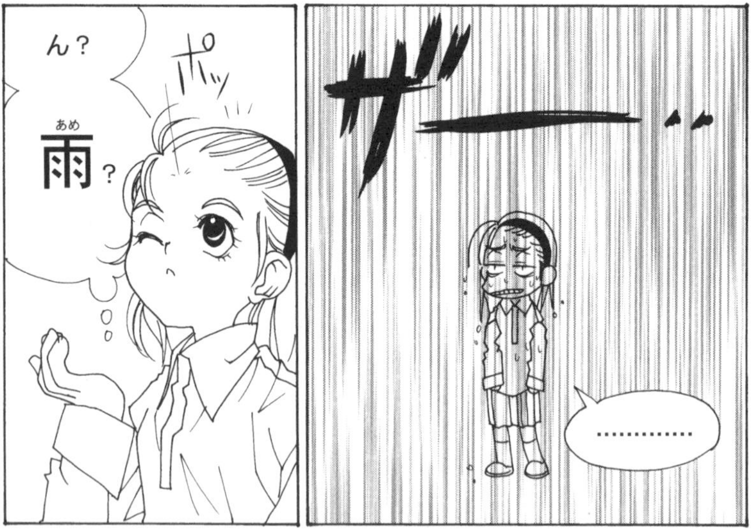
ん？
あめ
雨？
ポッ
ザー
....

Girl: ん？雨？。
Hmm. Rain?

ポッ
(sound of a single drop of rain)

ザー
(sound of heavy rain)

Girl: (speechless)

WHITE

しろ、しら、しろ(い)、ハク

ex. 白鳥* (はくちょう) - swan
ex. 白人 (はくじん) - Caucasian

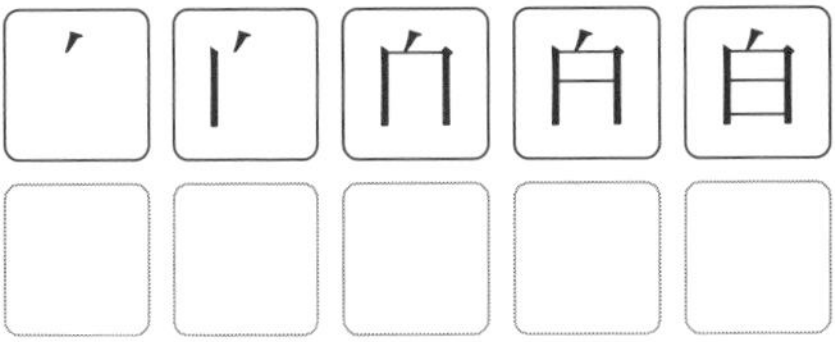

白

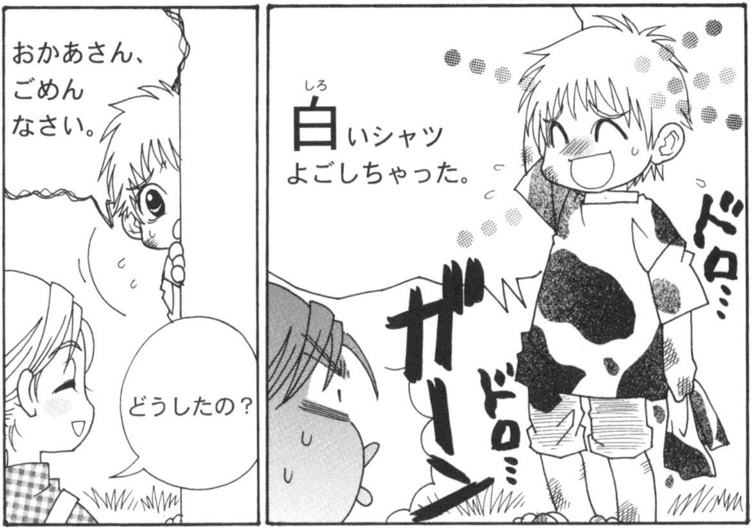

おかあさん、ごめんなさい。
どうしたの？
白(しろ)いシャツよごしちゃった。
ドロ
ガーン
ドロ

Boy: おかあさん、ごめんなさい。
Mom, I'm sorry.

Mother: どうしたの？
What's wrong?

Boy: 白いシャツよごしちゃった。
I got my white shirt dirty!

ガーン
(sound of realization)

ドロ　ドロ
(wet, muddy sound)

学

LEARN

まな(ぶ)、ガク

ex. 学生 (がくせい) - student
ex. 学年 (がくねん) - grade in school

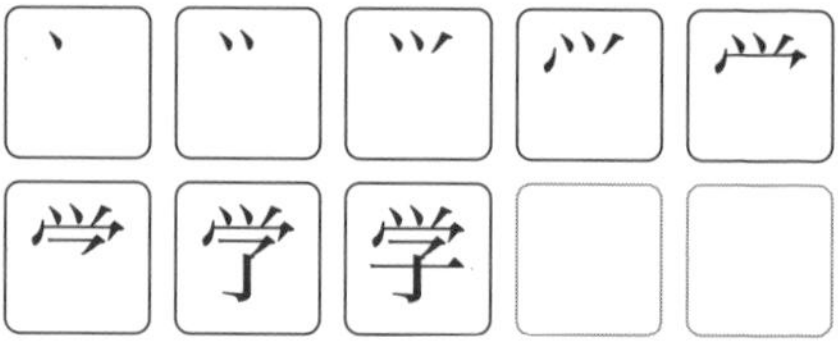

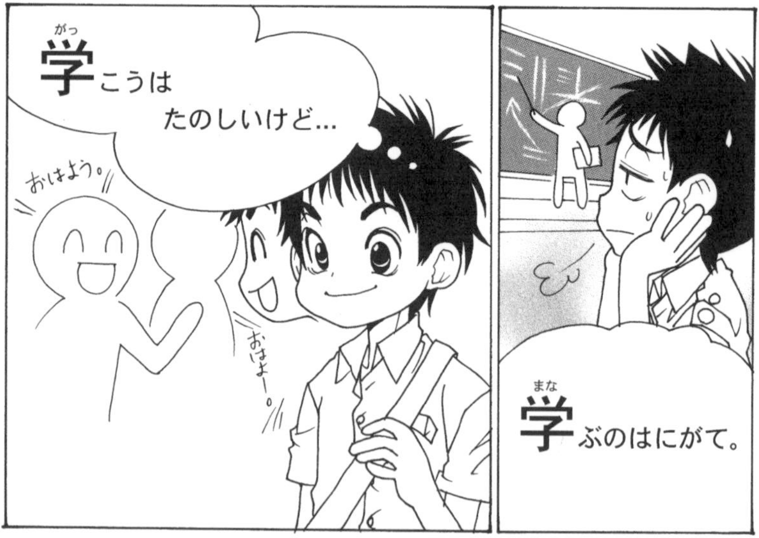

学こうは たのしいけど…
おはよう。
おはよー。
学ぶのはにがて。

Student: 学こうはたのしいけど…
School is a lot of fun, but...

Person in background: おはよう。
Good morning!

学ぶのはにがて。
Studying is a drag.

SCHOOL

コウ

ex. 学校 (がっこう) - school

ex. 校歌* (こうか) - school song

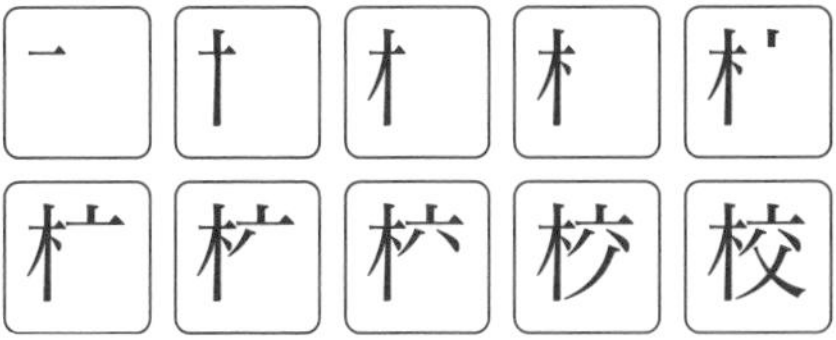

校

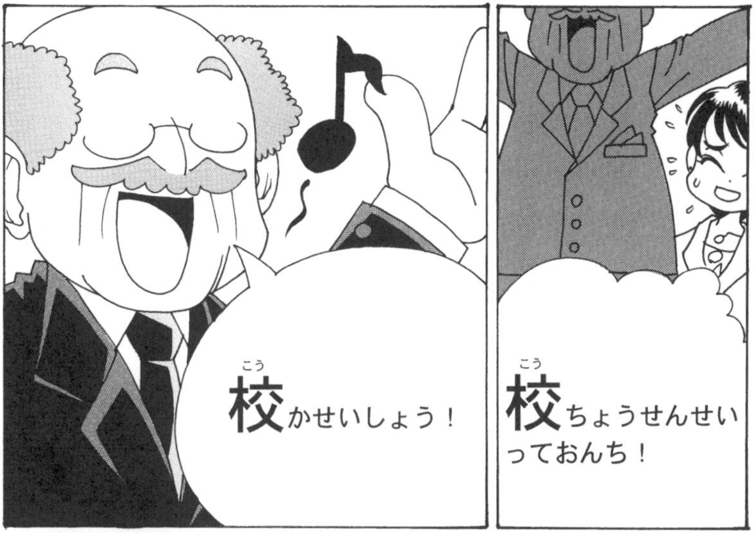
こう
校かせいしょう！
こう
校ちょうせんせいっておんち！

Principal: 校かせいしょう！
Let's sing our school song!

Student: 校ちょうせんせいっておんち！
The principal is totally tone deaf!

見

SEE

み(る)、み(える)、み(せる)、ケン

ex. 見本 (みほん) - sample
ex. 見学 (けんがく) - field trip

丨	冂	冃	月	目
目	見			

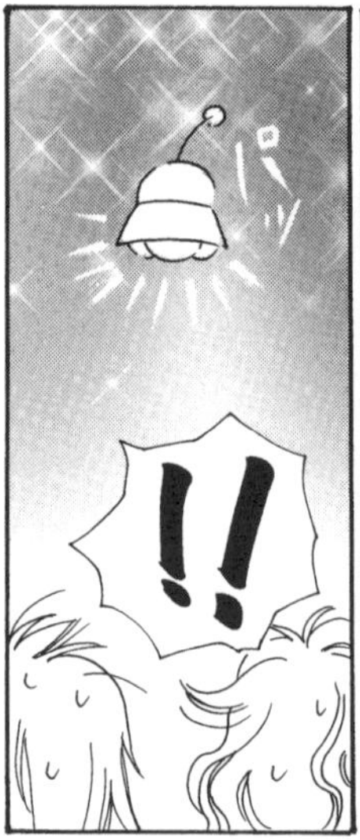
パッ
!!

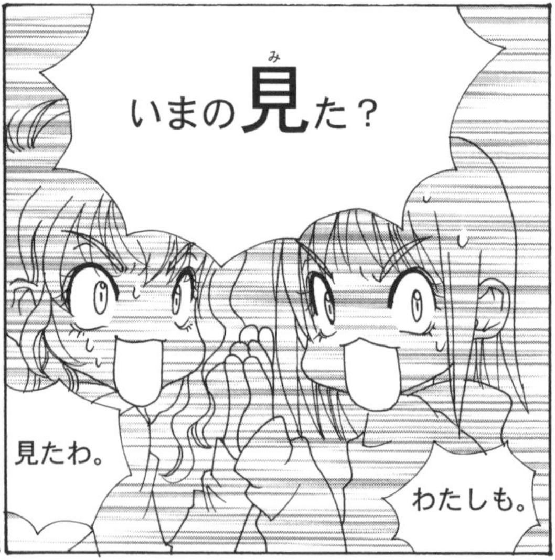
いまの見(み)た？
見たわ。
わたしも。

Girls (in unison after seeing UFO): いまの見た？
Did you see that?

Girl on left: 見たわ。
I saw it.

Girl on left: わたしも。
Me too.

HEAR

き(く)、き(こえる)、ブン

ex. 新聞* (しんぶん) - newspaper
ex. 聞き手* (ききて) - listener; audience
ex. 見聞 (けんぶん) - knowledge; information

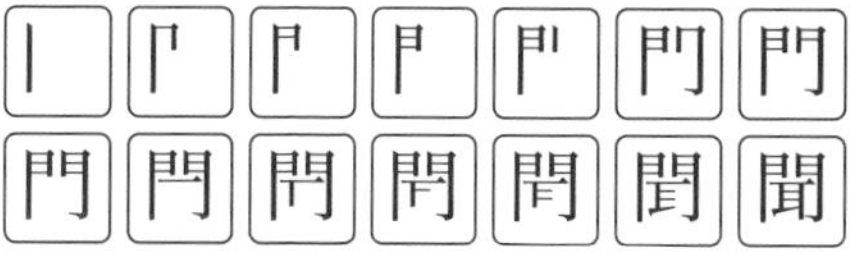

聞

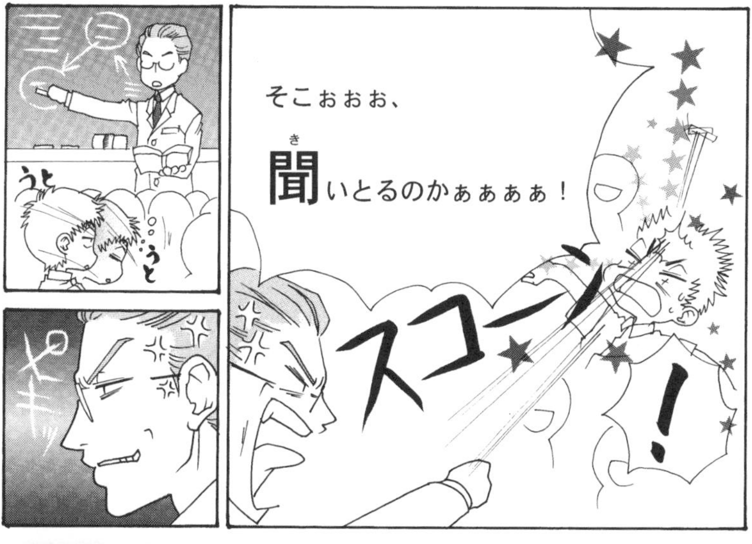
うと
うと
ピキッ
そこぉぉぉ、
聞(き)いとるのかぁぁぁぁ！
スコーン！

うと　うと
(sound of boy nodding off to sleep)

ピキッ
(sound of teacher noticing boy)

Teacher: そこぉぉぉ、聞いとるのかぁぁぁぁ！
Are you listening to me?!

スコーン
(sound of boy being hit by teacher's pointer)

話

SPEAK / TALK

はな(す)、はなし、ワ

ex. 話 (はなし) - story, speech
ex. 電話* (でんわ) - telephone
ex. 会話* (かいわ) - conversation

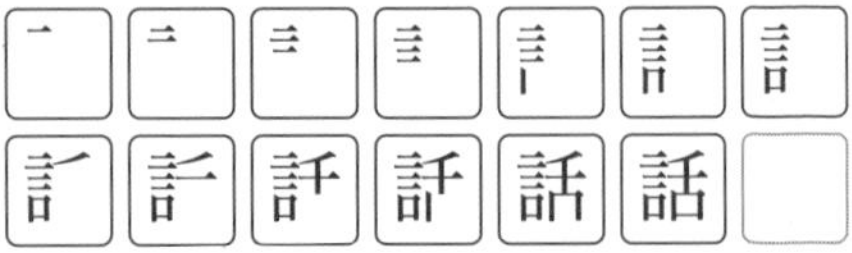

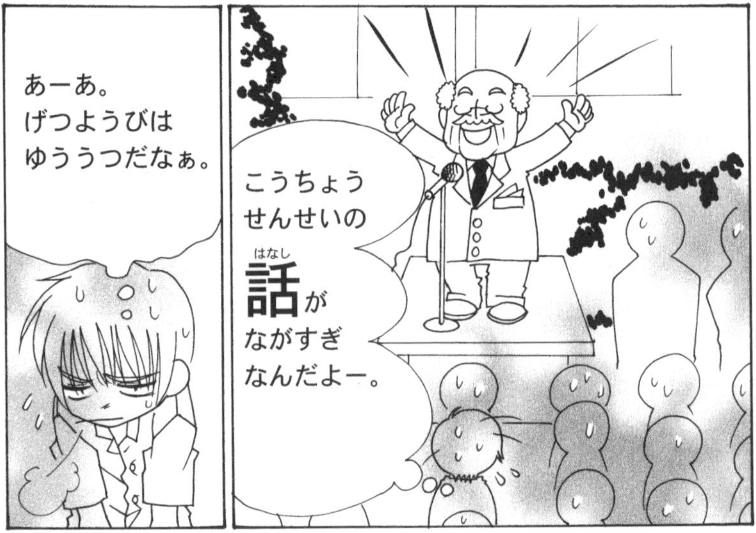
あーあ。
げつようびは
ゆうううつだなぁ。
こうちょうせんせいの話(はなし)がながすぎなんだよー。

Student: あーあ。
げつようびは
ゆうううつだなぁ。
Sigh...Monday's are such a drag.

こうちょうせんせいの話がながすぎなんだよー。
I swear the principal talks too much.

LANGUAGE

かた(る)、かた(らう)、ゴ

ex. 日本語 (にほんご) - Japanese language
ex. 英語* (えいご) - English language
ex. 語学 (ごがく) - linguistics

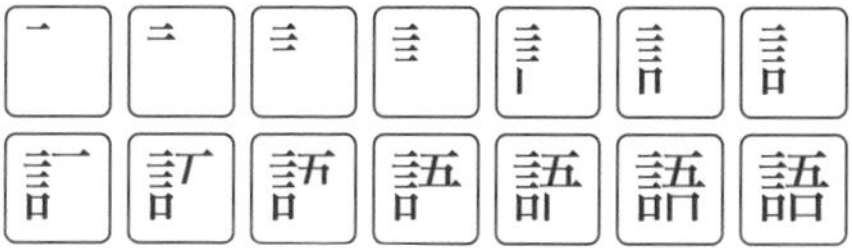

語

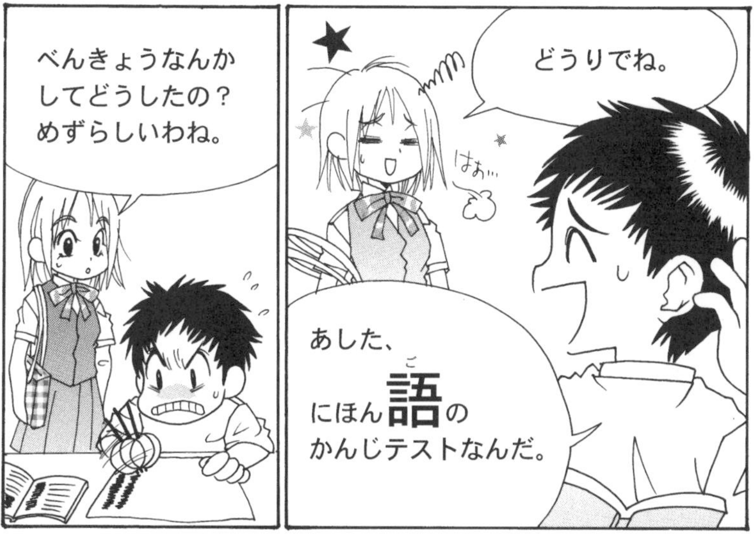
べんきょうなんかしてどうしたの？めずらしいわね。
あした、にほん語(ご)のかんじテストなんだ。
どうりでね。
はぁ…

Girl: べんきょうなんかしてどうしたの？めずらしいわね。
You're actually studying? What's up with that?

Boy: あした、にほん語のかんじテストなんだ。
I have a kanji test in my Japanese-language class tomorrow.

Girl: どうりでね。
That explains it.

読

READ

よ(む)、トウ、トク、ドク

ex. 読者 (どくしゃ) - reading book
ex. 音読み* (おんよみ) - on-reading (of kanji)
ex. 訓読み* (くんよみ) - kun-reading (of kanji)

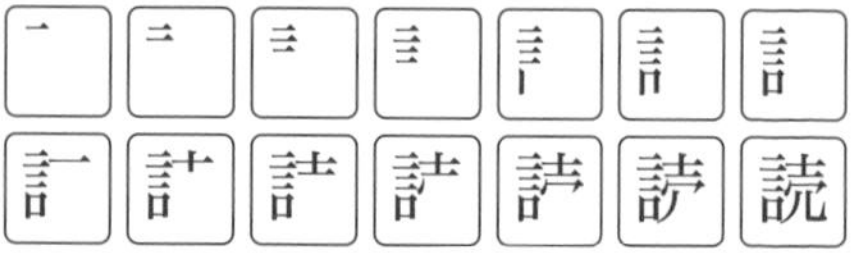

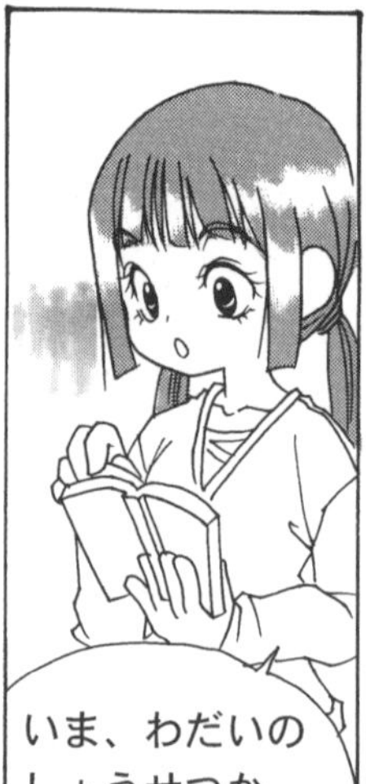
いま、わだいの しょうせつか。

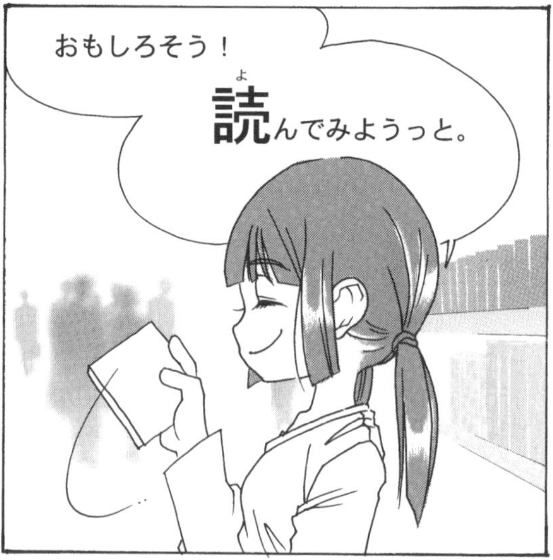
おもしろそう！ 読(よ)んでみようっと。

Girl: いま、わだいの しょうせつか。
So, this is that popular new novel.

おもしろそう！読んでみようっと。
Looks interesting. I'm gonna read it!

WRITE

か(く)、ショ

ex. 書道* (しょどう) - calligraphy
ex. 書店* (しょてん) - bookstore

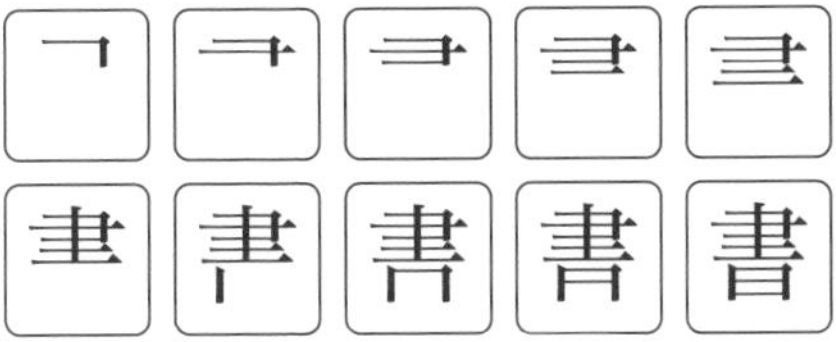

書

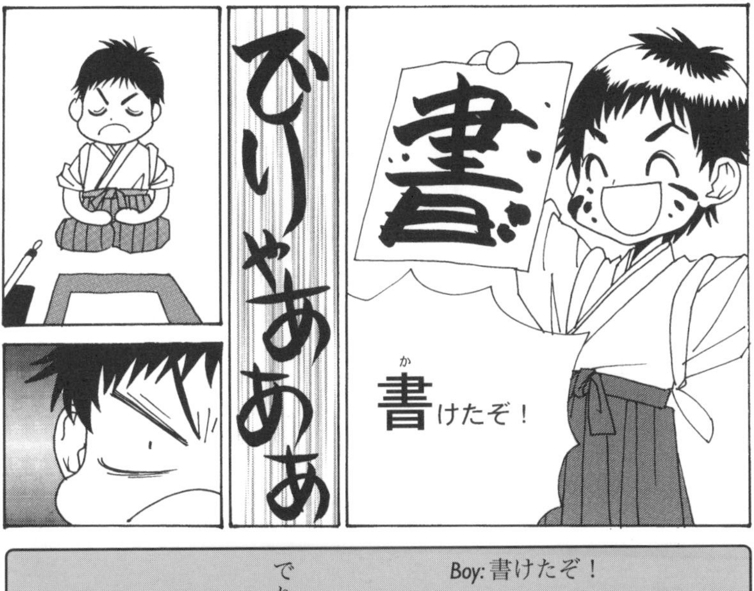
ひりゃあああ
書(か)けたぞ！

でりゃあああ
(Sound of furious writing)

Boy: 書けたぞ！
I've written my masterpiece!

食

EAT / FOOD

た(べる)、く(う)、ショク

ex. 食べ物* (たべもの) - food

ex. 食事* (しょくじ) - meal

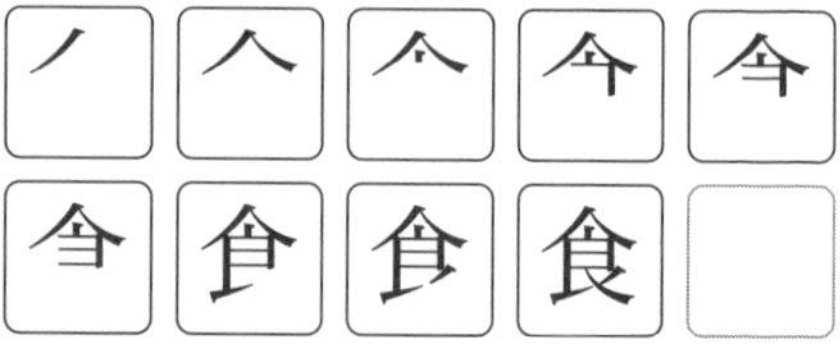

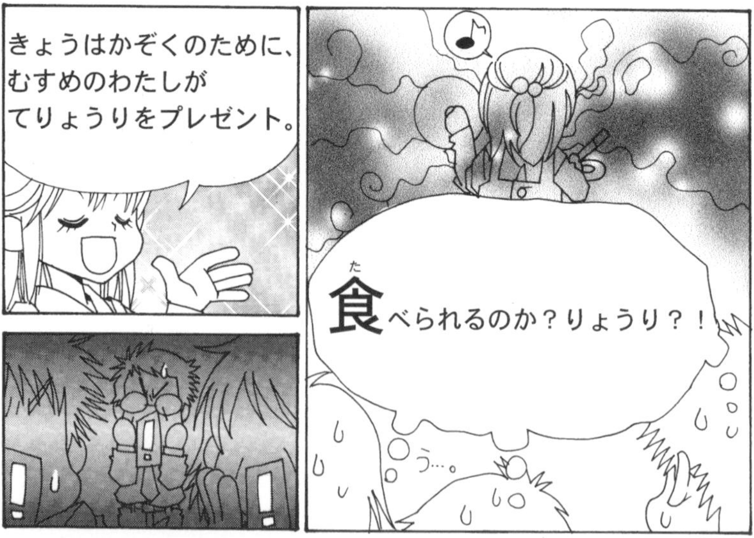
きょうはかぞくのために、むすめのわたしがてりょうりをプレゼント。
!
!
食べられるのか？りょうり？！
う…。

Girl: きょうは かぞくの ためにゝむすめのわたしが てりょうりをプレゼント。

Tonight, I, the loving daughter, shall make dinner for my family.

Family (thinking alike): 食べられる のか？りょうり？！

Will we be able to eat it?!

BOOK / MAIN

もと、ホン

ex. 絵本* (えほん) - picture book
ex. 日本 (にほん) - Japan

一	十	才	木	本

本

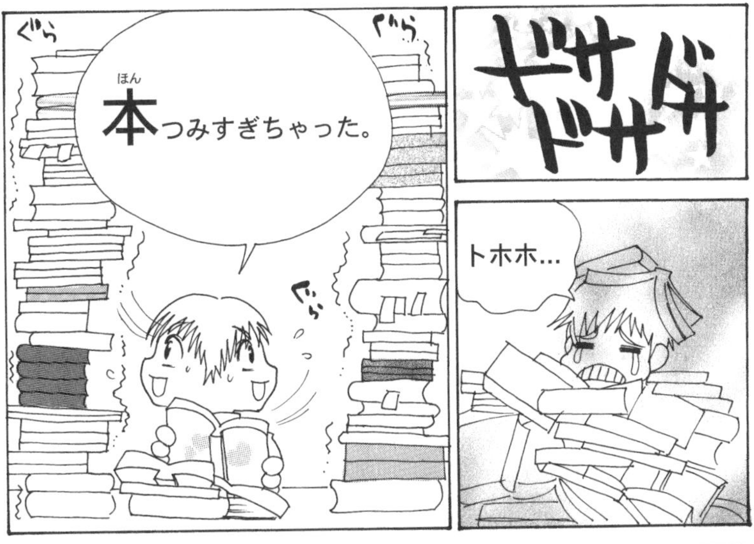
ぐら
ぐら
本つみすぎちゃった。
ぐら
ドサドサドサ
トホホ…

Schoolboy: 本つみすぎちゃった。
I've piled the books too high.

ぐらぐら (sound of shaking objects)

ドサ ドサ ドサ
(sound of falling objects)

トホホ…
Whimper...

ELECTRICITY

デン

ex. 電子 (でんし) - electronic
ex. 電子メール (でんしメール) - e-mail
ex. 電池* (でんち) - battery

Girl: わー！てい電。かいちゅう 電とうは？	Boy (in scary voice): こーこーに あーるーよー。
Yikes! A blackout. Where's the flashlight?	Heeeere it is.
	Girl: キャー
パッ	Eeeek.
(shining light)	ポウ...
	(shining light)

VEHICLE / WHEEL

くるま、シャ

車

ex. 車 (くるま) - car

ex. 電車 (でんしゃ) - train

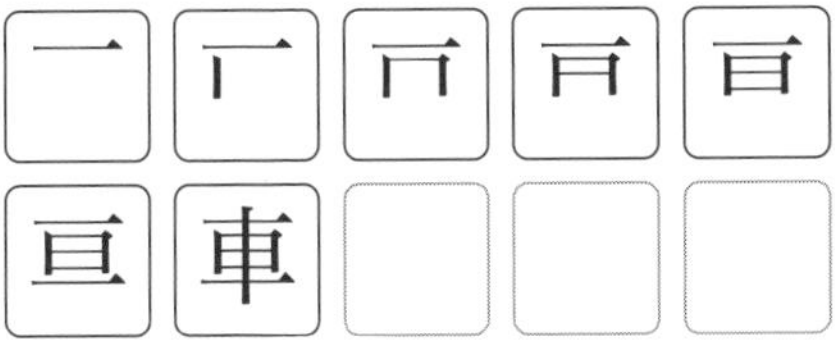

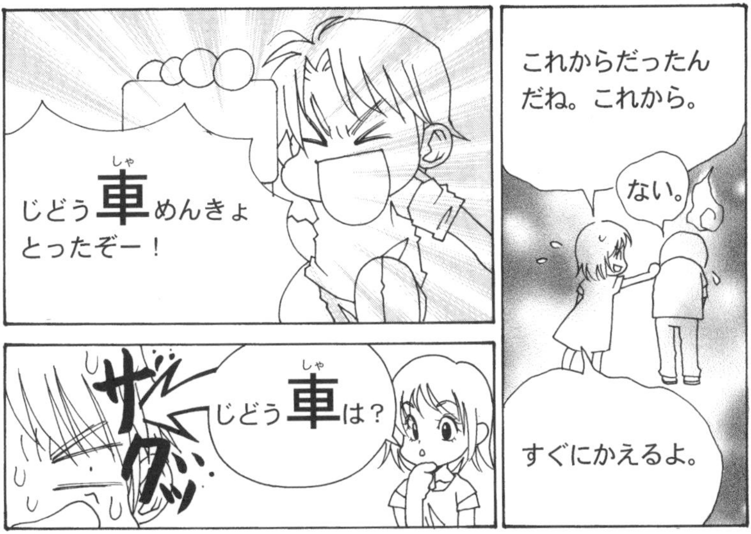
じどう車めんきょとったぞー！
ザグッ
じどう車は？
これからだったんだね。これから。
ない。
すぐにかえるよ。

Boy: じどう車めんきょとったぞー！
I just got my driver's license!

Girl: じどう車は？
You have a car?

ザグッ
(sound of sudden realization)

Girl: これからだったんだね。これから。すくにかえるよ。
One step at a time. You'll be able to buy one soon.

Boy: ない。
...no car...

名

NAME

な、メイ、ミョウ

ex. 名前 (なまえ) - name
ex. 名刺* (めいし) - business card

ノ	ク	タ	タ	名
名				

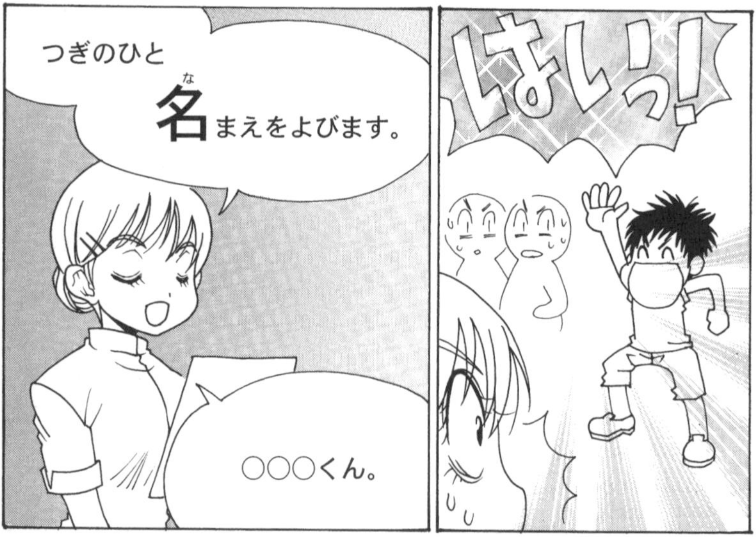
つぎのひと
名(な)まえをよびます。
○○○くん。
はいっ!

Teacher: つぎのひと名まえをよびます。
○○○くん。
I'm going to read the next person's name.
Mr._ _ _.

Boy: (answering before his name is called): はいっ!
Here!

The use of circles (as above) is common in Japanese manga, and is equivalent to the use of underlines in English to mean "fill in the blanks."

COUNTRY

くに、コク

ex. 外国 (がいこく) - foreign country

ex. 入国 (にゅうこく) - to enter a country

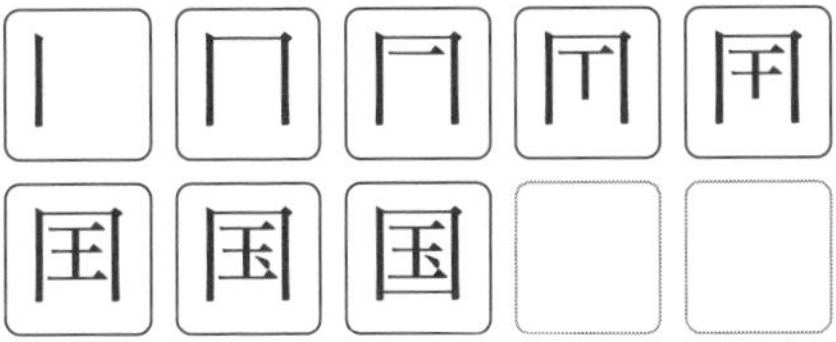

国

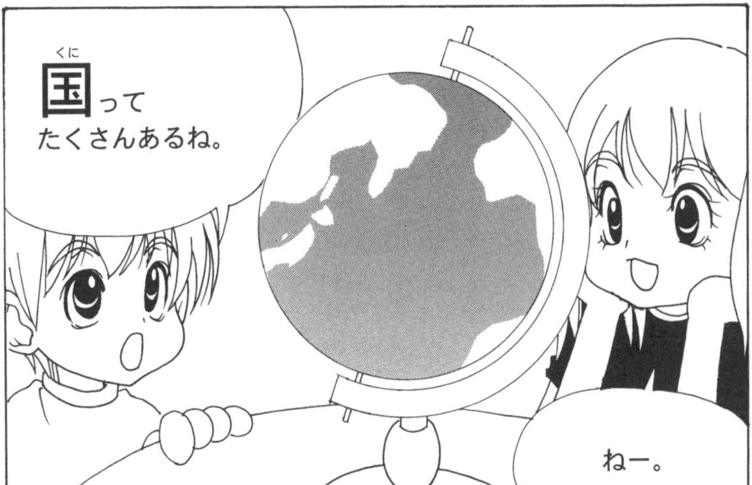
国(くに)って
たくさんあるね。
ねー。

Boy: 国ってたくさんあるね。
There sure are a lot of different countries!

Girl: ねー。
Yep.

TAKE THE TEST!

The Japanese Language Proficiency Test has been held annually throughout the world since 1984. Administered by the Japanese government and the nonprofit Japan Foundation, the test evaluates and certifies the proficiency of non-native speakers of Japanese. There are four levels to the examination: Level 4 for beginners, Level 3 for intermediate students, Level 2 for those who are functionally literate in Japanese, and Level 1 for experts.

This book includes all 80 kanji students need to know to pass Level 4 of the JLPT. Subsequent volumes in the "Kanji de Manga" series will help students prepare for the higher levels.

For more information about the Japanese Language Proficiency Test, including examination locations in your country, please visit the Japan Foundation's "JLPT Communications Square" website at http://momo.jpf.go.jp/jlpt/e/about_e.html.

Kanji de Manga

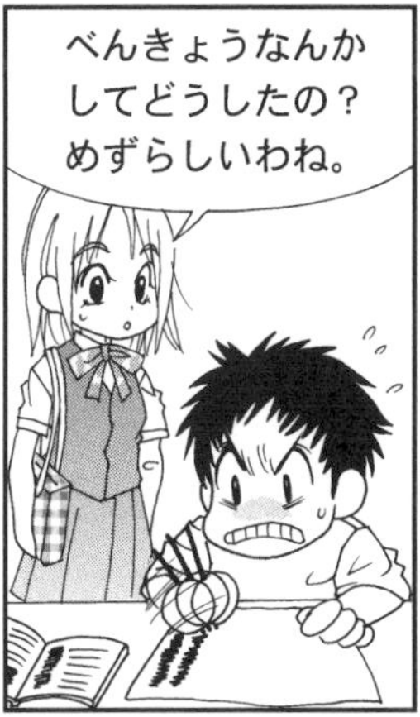
べんきょうなんか
してどうしたの？
めずらしいわね。

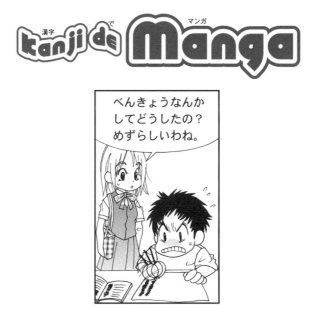

PRACTICE SECTION

ISBN 4-921205-03-5

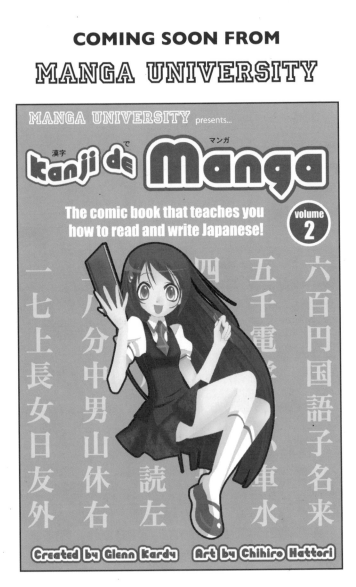

KANJI STROKE-ORDER RULES

The Golden Rule: "Left to Right, Top to Bottom"

1. Horizontal strokes: left to right and parallel to one another

2. Vertical/slanting strokes: top to bottom

3. Hook strokes: top left to right and turn to the bottom

4. Center strokes first, then slanting left and right strokes

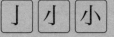

5. Outside strokes before inside strokes (but bottom stroke last)

6. Crisscross strokes: horizontal strokes first, vertical strokes second

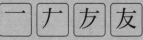

7. Diagonal strokes: left-hand first, right-hand second

8. Horizontal and vertical cutting strokes last